GOOD HOUSEKEEPING

Everyday Cook Book

A Combined Memorandum Cook Book and Scrap Book

ARRANGED BY

Isabel Gordon Curtis

Associate Editor of Good Housekeeping

Hearst Books
A Division of Sterling Publishing Co., Inc.
New York

Originally published and copyrighted in 1903
by The Phelps Publishing Co.

Published by Hearst Books,
A Division of Sterling Publishing Company, Inc.
387 Park Avenue South, New York, N.Y. 10016

Good Housekeeping and Hearst Books are trademarks
owned by Hearst Magazines Property, Inc., in the USA,
and Hearst Communications, Inc., in Canada.

www.goodhousekeeping.com

Distributed in Canada by Sterling Publishing
c/o Canadian Manda Group, One Atlantic Avenue,
Suite 105 Toronto, Ontario, Canada M6K 3E7
Distributed in Australia by
Capricorn Link (Australia) Pty. Ltd.
P.O. Box 704, Windsor, NSW 2756 Australia

Manufactured in China

10 9 8 7 6 5 4 3 2 1

Sterling ISBN 1-58816-210-9

Introduction

This work presents several new ideas in cook books. The size is extremely handy. It will lie open without taking too much room. The blank pages permit one to copy in or paste into its appropriate place the recipes of each particular kind of dish.

This memorandum feature alone has made the Good Housekeeping Everyday Cook Book extremely popular. The memorandum pages will also be particularly popular with subscribers to Good Housekeeping, who will now be able to put into this book in proper place all their favorite recipes from Good Housekeeping month by month.

Each and every recipe herein has been repeatedly tested in the experience of its originator. It has also been tested by various committees among the subscribers to the magazine Good Housekeeping. Finally each recipe as here printed has also been verified and tested by the New England School of Cookery.

These recipes represent the everyday routine of cookery, by many of the best cooks and housekeepers at home and abroad. It is in fact, as in name, an EVERYDAY cook book.

CONTENTS

A Few Rules

To Be Observed in Cooking from Recipes in This Book.

All measurements are level. A cup is the glass measuring cup marked with thirds and quarters. When it is full, it is leveled off smoothly with a dry knife.

When flour is to be measured in cupfuls, sift it, then lift with a spoon into a cup. Do not shake or press it down, simply make it full, then run a spatula over the top to level it.

A tablespoon of butter is measured in the same way. A tablespoon of melted butter means butter melted before measuring.

One cup of cream, whipped, means cream measured before whipping. Whipped cream requires measuring after being whipped.

Good Housekeeping Table of Weights and Measures

When recipes are found which deal with pounds and ounces, and scales are not at hand, the weights may be translated into level measurements, such as are used wholly in the New England School of Cookery. This is easy to do when one knows corresponding amounts. By level measurements are meant a spoon or cup filled full with dry material, then leveled off smooth, as shown in the illustration. Flour is sifted before being lifted into the cup or spoon, then leveled, and butter is packed in solid. Use always a measuring cup divided into thirds and quarters.

2	Cups	Lard	Make	1	Pound
2	"	Butter	"	"	"
4	"	Pastry or Bread Flour	"	"	"
3⅞	"	Entire Wheat Flour	"	"	"
4½	"	Graham Flour	"	"	"
4⅓	"	Rye Flour	"	"	"
2⅔	"	Corn Meal	"	"	"
4¾	"	Rolled Oats	"	"	"
2⅔	"	Oatmeal	"	"	"
4⅓	"	Coffee	"	"	"
2	"	Granulated Sugar	"	"	"
2⅔	"	Powdered Sugar	"	"	"
3½	"	Confectioner's Sugar	"	"	"
2⅔	"	Brown Sugar	"	"	"
2	"	Chopped Meat	"	"	"
1⅞	"	Rice	"	"	"
2	"	Raisins (packed)	"	"	"
2¼	"	Currants	"	"	"
2	"	Stale Bread Crumbs	"	"	"
9	Large Eggs		"	"	"
2	Tablespoons	Butter	"	"	Ounce
4	"	Flour	"	"	"
6	"	Baking Powder	"	½	"
3	Teaspoons		Make	1	Tablespoon
16	Tablespoons Dry Ingredient		Make	1	Cup

General Remarks

All foods are divided into two classes: the nitrogenous, or those which contain nitrogen, and the non-nitrogenous, or those that do not contain nitrogen. The nitrogenous are divided into two classes, the albuminoids or proteids, and the gelatinoids. The principal proteids are found in eggs, fish, meat, casein of milk, fiber of lean meat and the gluten of wheat. The white of an egg is almost entirely albumen. In the body these go to the formation and repair of tissue waste, the regulation of absorption and the utilization of oxygen. They may form fat, and they are partially converted into peptones in digestion.

The second division, or gelatinoids, are found in the collegan, or the gelatin of cartilage, and the ossein, or the gelatin of bones. These have the same function in the body as the proteids, but less perfectly. It is this form of food which gives the jelly-like consistency to our soup stocks.

The non-nitrogenous foods are divided into three classes: the carbohydrates, the hydrocarbons and the vegetable acids. The carbohydrates consist of starch, dextrine, cellulose, cane sugar, maltose, lactose, dextrose and levulose. All of these supply heat and energy by oxidation, or burning; supply fat by reducing the burning of the proteids, and are converted into dextrose during digestion. Digestion begins in the mouth, where the starch is changed to a form of sugar by the action of the ptyalin of the saliva. The final condition of all starch in digestion is dextrose.

The hydrocarbons consist of fats and oils. The fats are composed of three fatty acids: olein, the fatty acid of lard; stearin, or the fatty acid of suet; palmitin, or the fatty acid of butter   All of these supply heat and energy by burning or oxidation, and they also supply fatty tissue.   The oils are known as fixed or volatile.   The fixed oils are those that leave a stain, as olive oil, and the volatile oils are those which evaporate, as the essences.   These oils have the same functions as the fats.

The third division, or vegetable acids, are found in the fruits; oxalic, or the acid of rhubarb; tartaric, or the acid from grapes; citric, found in lemons; malic, found in tomatoes; acetic, found in vinegar, and lactic, found in sour milk. All of these preserve the alkalinity of the blood.

The minerals consist of the salts, chlorides, phosphates, etc, and these have various uses.   Water is nature's great solvent and carrier of food and waste products.

CARE OF THE PANTRY

Neatness and order in your pantry will depend in great measure upon the way you clear your table.   If you look upon the pantry as a dumping ground, then dirt and disorder will be inevitable, but if on the contrary you consider it a workshop to be kept shipshape you will avoid these dangers.   Shipshape means a place for everything and everything in its place.

Make up your mind in the beginning where you want to lay your knives, where you want your silver, the best place for your heavy and delicate china, and when these places are well chosen, then stick to them.   Keep the shelves well dusted and every drawer clean and in order.

You must be sure to have a bowl or pan large enough to hold all the broken bits of bone and scraps from each meal. A large yellow bowl or agate pan is the most suitable for this.   Do not use tin, as a piece of lemon or a spoonful of tomato will rust it and it will soon become disagreeable.

Do not begin your work until the food is put away. Next, empty every glass, cup, bowl and pitcher. Rinse with cold water those which have been used for milk, cream or wine. Scrape dishes carefully and put those of one kind together. This saves time, it does not waste it. A bit of bread from the broken bits will wipe out a fine china bowl or a silver ladle without scratching it as a knife would do. Always remove at once any food that has dropped on the floor, then you will have one less grease spot to clean. When you have finished washing the dishes, always leave your pan or sink perfectly clean. You will find it very easy by using sapolio.

Once a week, you must wash down the pipes with a strong solution of salsoda and water that is actually boiling, not simply hot. Never leave soiled towels lying in the pantry. After each meal, wash out those you have used and hang them to dry. You may add a little diluted ammonia to the water and if you will provide yourself with a small sized washboard, which you can buy for 25 cents, you will find the work will be made very much easier. Once a week all towels that have been used should be thoroughly boiled and ironed. You need fresh ones each time for the glass and fine china, so do not let your supply of fresh ones get exhausted before you have other ones to take their place.

See that the knife cleaner and silver cleaning materials are in their proper place. Keep hand towels and dish towels separate. Keep salad cloths by themselves. Be sure that the broom and long duster are hung, not left standing on the floor, and choose a good place for keeping dusting cloths and small feather dusters.

THE WASHING OF DISHES

Miss Downing says: "I have found in my teaching that only the pupils who do not know how to wash them properly dislike the washing of dishes. When I hear a young lady say, 'I hate to wash dishes,' I know she is not a trained worker and does not know the best ways of doing things."

Before you begin to wash at all, arrange a good dry place to put your dishes when they are dry. Arrange so that you have room enough without letting clean dishes touch soiled ones or being obliged to put dry dishes on a wet spot. Begin with the glass and see that every glass is emptied before you begin to wash. Cold water in one, some milk in another, claret in another, will soon make your dish water unfit to wash anything in. After the glass, take the delicate china cups and saucers, dessert plates, etc.

Put your mind on your work. See carefully each piece before it leaves your hand that it is clean and dry. By the time the glass and fine china are washed, the water will be chilled, so either throw it out and make a fresh suds for the silver or put it on the stove to reheat, while putting the clean dishes away. When your silver is dry, put it away. Do not let it lie where it will be spattered from the washing of the next things.

Now use your own judgment and see whether the water is clean enough and hot enough for the dishes. Never put many dishes to wash in at one time. Put dishes of one kind in at one time and dishes of another kind in at another time.

There is economy in the washing of dishes, as well as in everything else, and my experience has been that the best way of doing it is to make a hot suds in one pan, have a second pan half filled with very hot water and as the dish is washed in the suds, put it right through the hot water, thus making sure that every part is rinsed, then allow to drain on the draining board, or in another pan. By the time a panful of dishes are washed,

rinsed and drained, they are still hot
enough to wipe and you will not need
more than one or two towels. In making
the suds, be careful that it is not too
strong, as too much soap quickly takes
off color and gilding from the fine china,
and never leave the soap lying in the
water. Then you can work rapidly.
Change the water when it is necessary.

Never, on any account, leave the dishes
lying in the water while you go to
attend to something elsewhere. To do
so injures the gilding and coloring.
Remember if you are quick, you can do
a great deal before the water cools and
you will have to change it only when it
is soiled. There is good reason for
washing dishes of one kind together,
aside from the question of cracking and
wiping. When they are washed and dry,
they are ready to put away without
further sorting.

Silver trays used at each meal should
be washed after each meal, just as reg-
ularly as a bread plate or crumb tray,
because you cannot serve a meal without
leaving soiled spots and finger marks.

Watch the inside of your pitchers.
Sediment from boiling water may be
easily removed the first day. After that,
twice the time at least will be needed to
make them clean. If clear water or hot
soap suds will not do it, use a little
sapolio.

When your dishes and silver are all
finished, cleanse your steel knives.
Never let the handles touch the water.
Hold them in your left hand and wash
the blades with your right. After they
are washed, scour the blades with bath-
brick or on an emery board. Let the
blade rest flat upon your board. This
prevents bending and the loosening the
handles. Once every week your silver
should be thoroughly polished and in
between times can be kept clean with a
chamois cloth.

A soft brush is required for cleaning
cut glass. A clean towel should be

spread on a tray and each piece should be placed on this as it is wiped. This precaution is especially necessary for dishes that are deeply cut on the bottom, for if placed on a polished surface, the moisture produces a white mark. Fine sawdust is a good thing for cut glass. After wiping it bury it in sawdust for an hour or more, or brush off with a soft brush. The sawdust should come from a non-resinous wood such as basswood or box. Dry after using.

USE OF STALE BREAD

Have a laundry bag made of white duck to hang in the kitchen, in which to keep all pieces of bread which come from the table without butter. When a number have been collected put into the dripping pan and carefully dry and brown in the oven. Roll them on a molding board until fine and sift through a very fine sieve. Keep in a glass jar or a tin can uncovered. If they are covered they will quickly become rancid, especially if there has been any butter on any of the pieces.

HOW TO COMBINE INGREDIENTS

Next to correct measuring comes the care in combining ingredients, a fact often overlooked by the inexperienced. There are three methods to be consid-ered—stirring, beating, cutting and fold-ing.

To stir, means to mix by using a circular motion, widening the circles to thoroughly blend the materials. This is the motion ordinarily used.

To beat, we continually turn the ingredients over and over so as to bring the under part to the surface. By beating we enclose a large amount of air into the mixture.

To cut and fold we combine two ingredients by the use of two motions—the one a repeated vertical downward motion of cutting, and second, by turning the ingredients over and over from the bottom, allowing the bowl of the spoon to touch the bottom of the dish each time. These two motions are repeated until the mixture is well blended.

By stirring, ingredients are blended; by beating, a large amount of air is enclosed, and by cutting and folding, the air already beaten in is carefully retained.

UTENSILS IN THE KITCHEN

In the furnishing of a home if there is one place that is neglected, it is the kitchen, as far as having utensils for making work lighter and easier is concerned. I cannot think the fault comes all from a lack of money as much as from lack of knowledge of the proper use of things. Utensils should be selected with as much care and thought as one would give to any other furnishings of the home. If the family is small, select small utensils, each with some definite purpose in view.

Of all the wares on the market, agate or aluminum are the most satisfactory, for they are light, durable, and easily cleaned and can be found in almost every article manufactured. Iron is durable, but heavy, and when not in use for a long time should be protected by oily or waxy surfaces to keep from rusting.

Acids should never be used in anything except glass, porcelain or granite. French chefs use copper and brass utensils, but they are very expensive, must be kept scrupulously clean, as they are easily affected by acids or alkali and all their salts are poisonous. Cleaned most easily with oxalic acid. Ammonia dissolves copper or brass.

Zinc is attacked by acids and alkali.

Lead is attacked by salt or any organic material. Organic matter in water causes the objection to lead pipes.

It is the lead in the solder that causes the objection to canned goods.

Sulphuric acid will clean spots caused by salt water. None of its salts are considered poisonous.

Bright surfaces retain heat, therefore all utensils to keep liquid hot must be bright as possible.

Dark surfaces radiate heat, so when the oven does not bake well on the bottom, use dark or old baking pans.

Wooden spoons are much nicer to use, as they make less noise while stirring. The slitted wooden cake spoons are considered better, as they enclose more air in the mixture while beating than an ordinary spoon would do.

Always use a silver fork for beating an egg instead of an iron one, as the phosphorus of the yolk attacks the steel and forms a disagreeable salt.

PATTY CASES AND RISSOLES—PAGE 218

PEAS IN TURNIP CUPS—PAGE 312

MUSKMELON FRAPPE—PAGE 126

INDIVIDUAL STRAWBERRY SHORTCAKES
—PAGE 144

DEVILED OYSTERS IN THE SHELL—PAGE 268

THE REAL BOSTON COOKIES—PAGE 36

DESTINED TO BECOME BOSTON COOKIES
—PAGE 36

WAFFLES—PAGE 4

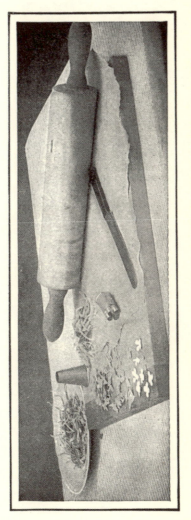

NOODLES IN PROCESS OF MAKING AND THE IMPLEMENTS THEREFOR—PAGE 290

CORN TIMBALES—PAGE 312

JELLY PRUNE RING—PAGE 84

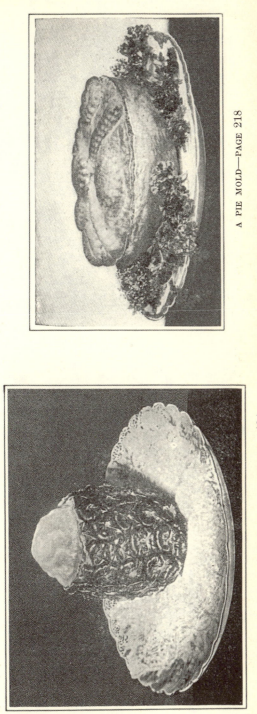

A PIE MOLD—PAGE 218

RASPBERRY CREAM IN PINEAPPLE SHELL—PAGE 124

XXI

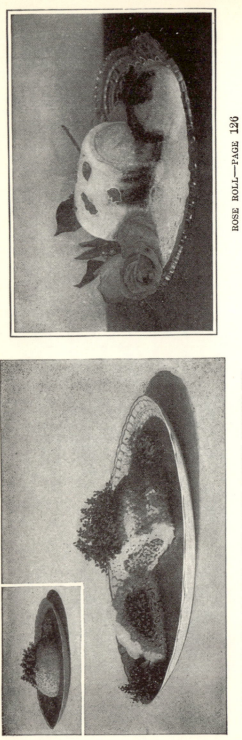

ROSE ROLL—PAGE 126

CASSEROLE OF RICE AND VEAL—THE LARGER PICTURE SHOWING THE
INTERIOR AFTER CUTTING—PAGE 198

SNOWBALL CROQUETTES—PAGE 178

xxiii

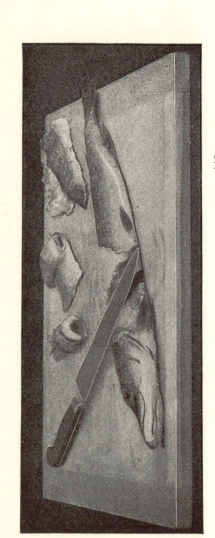

THE SKINNING AND FILLETING OF A FISH—PAGE 112

SWEDISH TIMBALES—PAGE 200

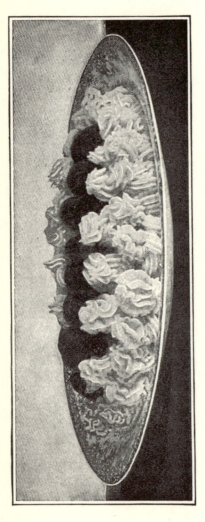

SAUSAGES AND POTATOES—PAGE 200

LOBSTER CREAM—PAGE 268

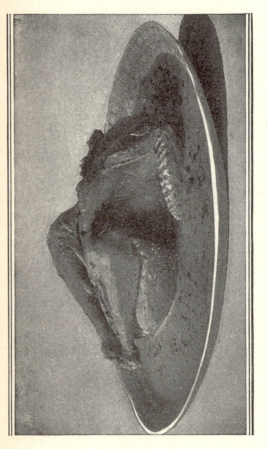

CHICKEN "A LA PROVIDENCE"—PAGE 200

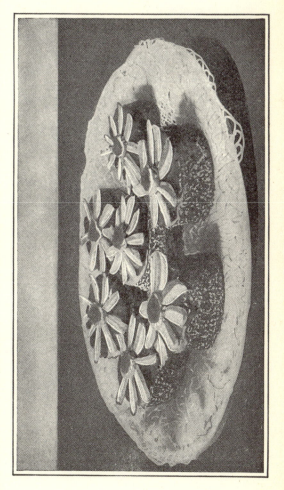

MARGUERITES—PAGE 52

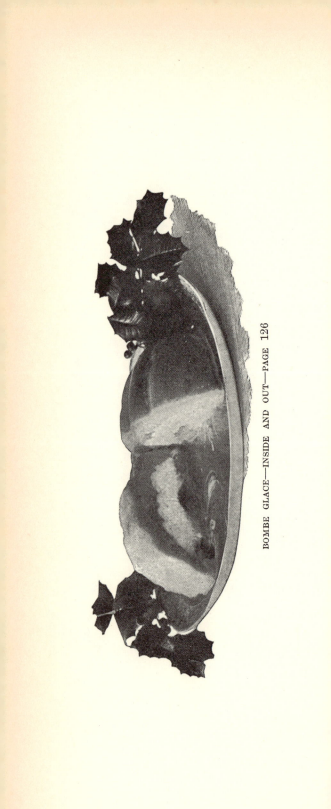

BOMBE GLACE—INSIDE AND OUT—PAGE 126

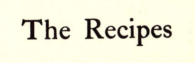

The Recipes

Baking Powder Breads

Popovers

Sift together one cup of sifted flour, one-fourth teaspoon of salt; gradually beat in a cup of milk and an egg beaten until light. Beat two minutes with a Dover beater, and bake about half an hour in a gem pan, buttered, in fast oven. —Mrs E. A. Wadhams.

Batter Cakes

Beat thoroughly one teaspoon of soda with one and one-half pints of sour milk. Beat the yolks of three eggs and add to the milk, then stir in the flour and a little salt, making the batter of the consistency of cake. Then beat the whites to a stiff froth, fold in, not thoroughly.—Mrs J. L. Brenner, Dayton, O.

Breakfast Puffs

Boil a pint of milk with a quarter of a pound of butter. Stir in three-quarters of a pound of flour and let cool. Beat the whites and yolks of five eggs separately and add. Fill greased cups half full of the batter, and bake in a quick oven. Turn out on a hot plate and sprinkle with sugar.

Flannel Cakes

Beat two eggs in a bowl and add a teaspoon of salt, a tablespoon of sugar and a pint and a half of milk, with a teaspoon of cream tartar and half a teaspoon of soda; add flour to make a thin batter. Bake on a greased griddle, spread with butter, and send to the table hot.

Snow Balls

Beat the whites of four eggs. Mix one cup of cream, two tablespoons of sugar, a teaspoon of baking powder and flour to make a batter, and add the whites of the eggs. Fill buttered cups two-thirds full of the mixture, and bake in a hot oven.

Peanut candy.

1 quart peanuts.
1 cup molasses.
1/2 " sugar.
1 tables. vinegar
1 heaping table s butter.
Add a little salt &
boil until candy is
hard when tried in
cold water. About
5 ms. before done,
stir in the nuts
& let them cook
until candy is done

Cream Waffles

Beat two eggs with a pint of sour cream; add a teaspoon of soda, half a teaspoon of salt, with flour to make a thin batter. Pour in well-greased waffle irons, bake brown, butter, and serve very hot.—See Page XVIII.

Scones

Sift one quart of flour; add half a teaspoon of salt, a teaspoon of sugar, a tablespoon of lard, one beaten egg, two teaspoons of cream tartar, one of soda and a pint of sweet milk. Mix to a thick batter, drop in squares on a very hot, greased griddle, and bake brown on both sides. Serve with butter and honey.

Buttermilk Biscuits

Sift a quart of flour, add a tablespoon of lard, half a teaspoon of salt, one teaspoon of soda, sour buttermilk to make soft dough, roll thin, cut into biscuits, and bake in a very quick oven.

Egg Biscuits

Sift a pint and a half of flour, add a teaspoon of salt, a tablespoon of sugar, two beaten eggs, a tablespoon of lard and half a pint of sweet milk to which has been added a teaspoon of cream tartar and half a teaspoon of soda. Work to a smooth dough, roll half an inch thick, cut out in large biscuits, rub over with sweet milk, lay on buttered tins and bake brown in a quick oven.— Eliza R. Parker.

Corn Cakes

Put a pint of meal in a bowl, mix through it a teaspoon of salt and pour over it enough fiercely boiling water just to moisten the mass; cover for five minutes or an hour, as convenient. Beat three eggs separately, add a cup of sweet milk to the yolks and pour over the scalded meal; mix well, add a teaspoon of baking powder or one-fourth of a teaspoon of soda and the beaten whites

Orange Marmalade,

1 Grape fruit -
1 Orange - 1 Lemon
Slice very thin.
Let stand in 12
cups water 24 hrs.
& then add 14 cups
sugar. Boil slowly
until firm enough -

of the eggs. The amount of boiling water for moistening will be about three-quarters of a pint. Neither the powder nor soda is really necessary, the cakes being quite perfect with only the lightening of the eggs. To bake, grease the griddle quite freely with sweet bacon or ham drippings, preferably. The batter, when put on, will spread out, sputter and form lacework edges (if it doesn't, thin it with more milk) and the cakes will be a little hard at first to turn, which must not be done until they are a rich brown all over. Put only three cakes on a plate, as they are too tender to separate at the table.

Hoecakes

Into one and one-third cups of meal mix a level teaspoon of salt and a rather heaping one of baking powder. Beat the yolks of two eggs until light, add a cup of sweet milk and pour the mixture over the meal, beating hard for a minute; now add the beaten whites. Put a tablespoon of lard in a spider and when it is hot, drop in the batter, making cakes about three inches long and three across. Brown on both sides and serve hot.

Corn Bread

One cup of meal, a level teaspoon of salt, a heaping one of baking powder, a tablespoon of butter (or lard), a cup and a half of sweet milk, and two eggs (three, when they are plenty, and then somewhat less baking powder). Mix the salt through the meal; beat the eggs until very light, without separating, add the milk and pour over the meal; mix well, sift in the baking powder and beat hard for two minutes, add finally the melted butter, pour into a baking pan and bake in a hot oven.—Ella Morris Kretschmar.

Boston Brown Bread

One cup of sour milk, one-half cup of New Orleans molasses, one egg, butter

size of walnut, one teaspoon of soda in the milk, and enough graham flour to thicken like cake. Steam three hours; start over cold water.—Mrs Orville Goren.

Rice Waffles

One and three-fourths cups of flour, two-thirds of a cup of cold boiled rice, one and one-fourth cups of milk, two tablespoons of sugar, one egg, two and one-half teaspoons of baking powder, one-fourth of a teaspoon of salt, one tablespoon of melted butter. Sift dry ingredients, work in rice, add milk, yolk of egg well beaten, and butter, then beaten white. Bake in waffle irons.

Spoon Bread (southern dish)

One pint of coarse white corn meal, one dessertspoon of salt, lard size of a walnut, one egg, whites and yolks beaten separately, and milk enough to make a very soft batter—so soft that it will be smooth when still—but not soft enough to separate if left standing. Buttermilk is better than sweet milk, in which case use one-half teaspoon of soda, depending on the acidity of the milk. If you use sweet milk, use two teaspoons of baking powder. Sift meal, put in salt and lard and moisten with hot water, not boiling, as that would spoil it. Warm water will swell the meal and prevent that dryness corn bread often has. Add milk and egg, and last of all the baking powder. If soda and buttermilk are used beat the soda into the buttermilk thoroughly, before adding to the meal. Last, but not least, put in a granite baking dish, well greased, and very hot, and bake at once in a hot oven.

Beverages

Ginger Pop

To two gallons of lukewarm water allow two pounds of white sugar, two lemons, one tablespoon of cream of tartar, a cup of yeast and two ounces of white ginger root, bruised and boiled in a little water to extract the strength. Pour the mixture into a stone jar and let stand in a warm place for twenty-four hours, then bottle. The next day it will be ready to "pop."

Cream Soda

One pound of loaf sugar, one pint of rich cream, one quart of water, one tablespoon of vanilla and one-quarter of an ounce of tartaric acid. Mix the ingredients and bring slowly to a boil, then put in jars. Use a tablespoon of this and a third of a teaspoon of soda to a glass of cold water.—M. F. Snider.

Orange Bouillon

The juice from enough fresh ripe oranges to make one quart of solid juice. Heat to boiling point, then add one tablespoon of dissolved cornstarch, and cook to a velvety cream. Add small dash of salt. Cool, then add one teaspoon of orange flower water and one teaspoon of orange curacoa. Serve in crystal soup bowls in finely cracked ice with a garniture of a few orange flowers and imported French wafers.—Annette Willing Carhartt.

Pineapple Punch

To make a fascinating violet-tinted punch of delicate flavor, put one cup of grated pineapple with one pint of water, cook for fifteen minutes. Strain through cheesecloth, pressing out all the juice. Add one pint of water and two cups of sugar, which have been boiled ten minutes, half a cup of freshly made tea, the

juice of three oranges and three lemons, one cup of grape juice and two and one-half quarts of water. Put in a punch bowl with a large lump of ice. Serve perfectly chilled in sherbet glasses.— Anne Warner.

Fruit Punch

Of the making of punches there is no end, but I give one which slips down with ease. Put one pint of water and one pound of sugar and the chopped yellow rind of one lemon on to boil. Boil five minutes, strain, and while hot slice into it two bananas, one grated pineapple and half a bottle Maraschino cherries and their liquor. When ready to serve put in the center of your punch bowl a square block of ice; pour over it two quarts of Apollinaris; add to the fruit the juice of six lemons and put it all into the bowl. Serve in thin, tall tumblers.—Anne Warner.

Egg Lemonade

Boil together two cups of sugar and three cups of water ten minutes. Add the grated rind of one lemon and the juice of three. Allow this to cool, and at serving time add one egg beaten until very light and creamy and one bottle of effervescent table water, poured from some hight in order that the mixture may foam. Serve with cracked ice in the glasses.

Chocolate Cream Nectar

This may be made either from cake chocolate or from any of the cocoa powders, and a trial will determine which is the more agreeable. Melt two squares of chocolate or an equivalent amount of cocoa powder in four tablespoons of hot coffee. Add one and one-half cups of sugar and three cups of water. Boil clear and strain. There should be one quart of the liquid. When cold add one tablespoon of sherry wine and pour iced into glasses in which you have placed one tablespoon of whipped cream, not too

stiffly beaten. Stir well before drinking. The wine may be omitted and one teaspoon of vanilla substituted. This is good hot if a portion of hot milk is added to the chocolate syrup, and the whipped cream placed on the top.

Iced Coffee with Orange Flavor

One quart of strong coffee and two cups of sugar boiled together ten minutes. Allow this to cool and add to each cup or glass one tablespoon of orange syrup and the same amount of cream partially whipped. The orange syrup may be obtained at the drug store or made by allowing cut oranges to stand in sugar and straining off the juice. This may not sound promising, but a trial will convince the most skeptical. It was suggested to me by observing the toothsomeness of coffee ice cream and orange ice when served together.— Mrs E. B. Jones.

Black Currant Cup

To one quart of weak green tea add half a pint of black currant juice; sweeten to taste and chill thoroughly before serving.

Ching Ching

Fill a glass two-thirds full of shaved ice; add three or four lumps of sugar, the juice of a large orange and a few drops each of essence of cloves and peppermint.

Raspberry Shrub

Add to eight quarts of fine ripe black raspberries sufficient vinegar to reach the top, but not to cover them. Let stand in a stone jar for twenty-four hours. Then strain through a colander, mashing the berries well. Strain again through cheesecloth, and measure the juice. Allow one pound of sugar for one pound of juice. Put the juice in a preserving kettle and let it boil for twenty minutes; add the sugar and boil ten minutes longer. Seal in fruit jars or bottles.

Strawberry shrub may be made in the
same way.

Strawberry Punch

Boil a quart of water and two and
one-half cups of sugar for about ten
minutes, add one cup and a quarter of
strawberry juice, and cool. Before
freezing add half a cup of Maraschino
and it will then not freeze hard. Serve
in cups.—Anne Warner.

Fruit Cup

Take the juice of half a lemon, one
tablespoon each of lime and pineapple
juice, four ounces of sugar and half the
amount of shaved ice. Fill up the glass
with rich milk, shake until foamy and
drink at once.

Pineapple Lemonade

Pare, eye and grate a large ripe pineapple; add the strained juice of four
lemons and a syrup made by boiling together for four minutes one pound of
sugar and one pint of water. When cold
add one quart of water; strain and ice.

Raspberry Syrup

To each pint of strained raspberry
juice add one pound of granulated sugar.
Let it stand over night. In the morning
boil it for ten minutes and bottle. A
spoonful or two in a glass of cold water
makes a very refreshing drink.

Fruit Beverage

Peel twelve lemons very thin, squeeze
the juice over the peel and let stand two
hours, then add one pound of sugar.
Mash one quart of ripe raspberries with
half a pound of sugar; pare a ripe pineapple, shred the fruit fine and mix with
another half pound of sugar, then strain
the lemon juice and mash the raspberries
through a coarse sieve, then the pineapple, and mix all together, adding three
quarts of cold water. Stir until the
sugar is entirely dissolved, then strain,
and serve with a little of the fruit in each
glass.

Grape Shrub

Crush the grapes, put them in a stone jar and cover with good cider vinegar, and then cover the jar tightly. Press and stir the grapes frequently and let them stand three days. Then strain through folded cheesecloth two or three times, and to every three quarts of juice add five pounds of sugar. Stir until the sugar is dissolved; let come to a boil, skim carefully and bottle while hot. In serving allow two-thirds of water to one-third of juice.—M. F. Snider.

Bread Made With Yeast

Whole Wheat Bread

Scald one cup of fresh milk, add one heaping teaspoon each of butter, sugar and salt. When butter is melted, add one cup of cold water. When lukewarm, add one cup of warm water in which is dissolved one compressed yeast cake. Stir in three cups of good white bread flour; beat well, and set to rise, covered, in a warm place. Let rise from one to two hours till the sponge is full of bubbles. Then stir in sufficient whole wheat flour to make a dough that can be handled, and knead twenty minutes, using as little flour (entire wheat), as possible, as too much flour worked in makes heavy, tough bread. Let rise, and when light (from two to three hours in a warm place), mold lightly into loaves, and set to rise in three medium-sized greased bread tins. When light again, bake for about fifty minutes in a moderate oven. Started early in the morning, the baking can be accomplished by noon. If more convenient to set it at night, use only half a yeast cake, and after kneading, leave in a rather cool place, as too much rising will result in sour, worthless bread.—Jane Johnston.

Finger Rolls

Mix one cup of scalded milk with one tablespoon of butter. When cool, add one teaspoon of sugar, one-half teaspoon of salt, four tablespoons of liquid yeast (one-fourth cup), and flour enough to make a soft dough—about three cups. Mix well, knead for fifteen minutes and set in a warm place to rise for three or four hours. When light, knead again. Shape small pieces of dough into balls, then roll on the molding board into a small, long finger roll, pointing the ends. Place the rolls in a shallow pan, let them

rise for one hour, or until double in size, brush them over with a little beaten egg to give a glaze, and bake in a hot oven for ten or fifteen minutes.—Annabel Lee.

German Coffee Cake

Scald and cool to lukewarm one-half pint of milk. Add one heaping tablespoon of butter and two of sugar; one-fourth of a yeast cake dissolved in a little warm water, a speck of salt, and flour enough to make a soft bread dough. Let it rise over night; knead in the morning early, let it rise in a flat buttered tin. Rub butter over the top, sprinkle with sugar and cinnamon and bake for twenty to thirty minutes. Cut in squares and serve hot with coffee.— A. L.

Buns

Dissolve one cake of yeast in one pint of lukewarm water, add flour to make a moderately stiff sponge, let rise until it begins to drop (about two hours), rub together one-fourth pound of butter, one-fourth pound of sugar and two eggs, one cup of warm milk, a little salt, and add all to the sponge; let rise one hour, then mold, put in pans, let rise until light, and bake.—Mrs F. M. Hall, Lincoln.

Southern Sally Lunn

One quart of flour, three eggs, one teaspoon of butter, one teacup of yeast, one pint of new milk. Beat the yolks of eggs light. Stir in the yeast, then butter, milk and flour. Beat the whites light, and add last. Set to rise and bake in a pan or muffin rings when ready.—Mrs Charles Brinton Coxe, Philadelphia.

Bread in Five Hours

Scald one quart of milk and let cool to blood heat. Add two dissolved yeast cakes, two teaspoons of salt and two teaspoons of sugar. Use this for the wetting of the sifted flour, which should be of sufficient quantity to make a fairly

stiff dough. Let rise in a room where the temperature is 80 degrees, for four hours. Knead into small loaves, put into greased pans and let rise, then bake for half an hour. In the first mixing use a spoon and beat the dough vigorously to insure a perfect mixing of wetting and flour. In the kneading for the pans, work each loaf three or four minutes. This method insures the best bread ever eaten.—Mrs William A. Herron, Pittsburg.

Rye Bread

Mix one quart of milk, one quart of warm water, one-half cup of lard or butter, one yeast cake, one tablespoon of salt, one-third cup of sugar. After this is well mixed, add rye flour until it is as stiff as you can stir with an iron spoon. When light mold into loaves, using wheat flour for this purpose. Let it rise the second time in the tins until sufficiently light to bake. This bread is better not to rise too much and do not have too hot an oven.—Mrs Brewer.

Waffles

To serve five or six people, take four eggs, and to the beaten yolks add a little salt, a pint of milk and enough flour to make a stiff batter. After mixing these to a smooth consistency, thin the mixture by adding gradually the beaten whites of the eggs and enough milk to make it quite thin enough to pour from a teacup, adding half a teaspoon of yeast powder. Have the waffle pan thoroughly hot and well greased with lard, and pour the batter in from a cup.

Nut Bread

Set a sponge of one cup of entire wheat flour, one cup of white flour, one-half cake of compressed yeast, one cup of milk. When light add two tablespoons of brown sugar, one teaspoon of salt, one-quarter pound of shelled hickory nuts and enough entire wheat flour to make stiff as can be stirred with

spoon. Put in pan, let rise for one hour and bake one hour.—Mrs Charles Brantingham, Rockford.

Raised Oatmeal Muffins

To three-fourths of a cup of scalded milk add one-fourth of a cup of sugar and half a teaspoon of salt. When lukewarm, add one-fourth yeast cake dissolved in one-fourth cup warm water. Work one cup cold cooked oatmeal into two and a half cups of bread flour. Combine the mixtures, beat thoroughly and let the batter rise over night. In the morning fill buttered gem pans two-thirds full. Let it rise again and bake for twenty-five or thirty minutes in a moderate oven.

Cakes, Cookies, Dough-nuts, Etc

Spanish Chocolate Cake

Dissolve on the back of the stove half a cup of grated unsweetened chocolate, one-fourth of a cup of granulated sugar and two tablespoons of milk. Beat to a cream one-third of a cup of butter and a cup of powdered sugar; add two eggs, one at a time, beating well, and half a teaspoon of vanilla; next add the dissolved mixture and beat thoroughly; now add gradually one-fourth of a cup of milk, a cup of flour and a teaspoon of baking powder, the baking powder mixed with a little of the flour and added last. Bake in an oblong sheet about three-quarters of an inch thick. Place an ounce of unsweetened chocolate in a small teacup, and stand this in a pan containing boiling water, to melt it. Boil together until it forms a soft ball when dropped in cold water, a cup of granulated sugar and five tablespoons of milk; take from the fire, add vanilla to flavor and beat until white, yet soft and creamy; spread smoothly on the cake at once, while the cake is yet warm; then coat immediately with the melted chocolate, using preferably a soft pastry brush, although a knife will serve the purpose. Cut the cake in squares or diamonds and serve the same day it is made. This is a very choice recipe, making an elegant cake. — Amelia Sulzbacher.

Pound Cake as Our Mothers Made It

One pound of flour, one pound of butter, one pound of sugar, ten large eggs and about one-fourth of a nutmeg. Cream the butter and sugar together well (our mothers' rolled and sifted loaf sugar is better, but granulated sugar will

answer the purpose), then add the well-beaten yolks of the eggs, and add the flour, a little at a time, beating very thoroughly all the while, lastly add the whites of the eggs which have been beaten to a stiff froth that can be cut with a knife, or that will adhere to the vessel in which it has been beaten, being careful not to beat the cake after the whites have been added, but merely to fold in the puff. Flavor with one-fourth of a grated nutmeg, which should be put in before the whites of eggs. Bake in a very moderate oven for one hour. The only improvement that could be made on this recipe would be to use pastry flour (which was not used in mother's time). The best authorities on cake baking declare that good results cannot be obtained without the use of pastry flour.—Mrs P. L. Sherman, Chicago.

Orange Cake

Two cups of sugar, two and one-quarter cups of flour, one-half cup of water, yolks of five eggs, whites of four eggs, grated rind of one orange, one teaspoon of cream tartar, one-half teaspoon of soda. Bake in four tins.

Filling: Whites of two eggs, add pulverized sugar till stiff, the grated rind of one orange and the juice of two, to which add sufficient sugar to spread. —Mrs J. B. Hobbs, Chicago.

Extra Nice Walnut Cake

Beat to a cream one-half cup of butter and one cup of sugar. Dissolve one-half cup of cornstarch in one-half cup of milk, and add to butter and sugar, then add one cup of flour with one teaspoon of baking powder and the whites of two eggs beaten stiff. At the last add one cup of chopped walnut meats, and flavor with vanilla.

Cocoanut Loaf Cake

One cup of sugar, one-half cup of butter, three-quarters cup of milk, three

eggs, two and one-half cups of flour, two
teaspoons of baking powder and one
grated cocoanut. Cream the sugar and
butter, take the milk of the cocoanut and
if not enough add sweet milk to make
the three-quarters of a cup. Add the
beaten yolks, then flour and baking
powder sifted, then beaten whites, and
lastly the grated cocoanut, reserving
some for the frosting of the loaf. This
is to be baked in a deep tin.—Mrs George
Brewer.

Longmeadow Loaf Cake

Cream five cups sugar, one and one-half
cups butter, one cup lard. Mix thoroughly, divide and to the smaller part
of this mixture add four cups of warm
milk, one cup of distillery yeast and
flour enough to make batter which will
be hard to stir with a spoon. Let it rise
over night in a warm place. In the
morning add the rest of the sugar and
shortening, the whites of four eggs, one-
third cup of brandy, one teaspoon of
nutmeg and one teaspoon of saleratus.
Allow it to rise again until light, it may
take four hours, then add one and one-
half pounds of raisins and one-half
pound of citron. Put in six round tins,
and raise until light. Bake slowly one
hour.

An Historical Cake

An historical recipe for a great cake
"wrote by Nellie Custis for her grand-
mama." "Take forty eggs and divide
the whites from the yolks and beat them
to a froth. Then work four pounds of
butter to a cream and put the whites
of eggs to it, a spoonful at a time, till it
is well worked. Then put four pounds
of sugar finely powdered into it, in the
same manner, then put in the yolks of
eggs and five pounds of flour and five
pounds of fruit. Two hours will bake
it. Add to it one-half an ounce of
mace, one nutmeg, one-half pint of wine
and some fresh brandy."—Mrs Charles
Custis Harrison, Philadelphia.

Gingerbread

Three pounds of flour, one-half pound of butter, two tablespoons of ginger, two tablespoons of soda. Put the butter, flour and other ingredients together and mix as much molasses as will make a dough. Roll into thin sheets. Cut in any shape you fancy and bake in a moderate oven.—Mrs James T. Halsey, Philadelphia.

Crumpets

One cup of sugar, one-half cup of butter, one-half cup of milk, two cups of flour, a little vanilla, a teaspoon of baking powder. Spread with teaspoon on baking pan. When baked roll while hot into cornucopias or any shape desired.— Mrs Walter Snowdon Smith.

Delicious Raised Doughnuts

are made from one cup of sugar, one-half cup of butter, two eggs, one pint of warm milk, one cup of yeast, or one yeast cake dissolved in warm water, one-half teaspoon each of soda and salt, a dash of nutmeg. Mix with flour like soft bread dough, let it rise over night. Turn out on a floured board, roll out one inch thick without molding, cut into rings, let rise until very light. Fry in hot fat, turning often. When cold, roll in powdered sugar. If these doughnuts are kept in a jar and heated and rolled in sugar as they are needed, they will seem like freshly cooked doughnuts. Another way to have fresh doughnuts every day is to make the dough as directed and cut off enough each morning to roll out and fry for breakfast, keeping the rest of the dough on ice, which chills the yeast plant and retards rising. The cook must rise early to raise the dough. The first method is easier and the cakes are about as good. This recipe makes about four dozen medium-sized doughnuts.—Annabel Lee.

Dropped Hermit Cookies

One cup of butter, one and one-half cups of brown sugar, one cup of raisins

chopped fine, one cup of English walnuts chopped fine, one and one-third
cups of flour, three eggs, one teaspoon
of cinnamon, one teaspoon of cloves, one
teaspoon of allspice, one teaspoon of
salt, one teaspoon of soda in hot water.
Cream sugar and butter together, add
the other ingredients, and then put small
drops of the mixture in your pans for
baking.—Mrs G. Barrett Rich.

Boston Cookies

One cup of butter, one and one-half
cups of sugar, three eggs, one teaspoon
of soda, one and one-half tablespoons of
hot water, three and one-fourth cups of
flour, one-half teaspoon of salt, one teaspoon of cinnamon, one cup of chopped
walnuts, one-half cup of currants, one-
half cup of seeded chopped raisins. Cream
the butter, add the sugar gradually and
eggs well beaten. Add soda dissolved in
water, half the flour mixed and sifted
with salt and cinnamon, then add nut
meats, fruit and remaining flour. Drop
by spoonfuls one inch apart on a buttered sheet and bake in a moderate oven.
—Fannie M. Farmer. See Page XVIII.

Inexpensive Sponge Cake

One cup of granulated sugar, one and
one-half cups of flour with one scant
teaspoon of baking powder sifted together three times. Three eggs beaten
separately, one-half cup of cold water.
Pour about half the water on the sugar
and then add yolks of eggs well beaten;
add the remainder of the water and flour
alternately, then add whites of eggs, stir
lightly, put in pan and bake forty minutes.—Mrs J. H. Avery.

Maple Sugar Filling for Cake

Break into small pieces sufficient
maple sugar to make one cup. Put it
into a saucepan with one cup of sweet
cream and one cup of coffee sugar. Heat
slowly, stirring occasionally, until the
maple sugar is entirely dissolved. Boil
steadily without stirring until, when a

little is tried in very cold water, it can be rolled into a soft ball between the thumb and finger. Take at once from the fire, stir in a cup of chopped pecans, let stand for five minutes, then stir slowly until it begins to thicken, and spread between the layers of cake.

Maple Sugar Frosting

Add one cup of sweet cream to two cups of rolled maple sugar; boil slowly until it will thread from a spoon, about three-quarters of an hour. Then let it get about half cool, stir in half a cup of chopped English walnut meats, beat until it becomes creamy, then spread it over the cake.

Maple Sugar Cookies

One cup of sugar, one cup of crushed maple sugar, one cup of butter, two well beaten eggs, two tablespoons of water, two teaspoons of baking powder, and flour enough to roll out. Do not make too stiff. Bake in a quick oven.

English Banbury Cakes

Two pounds of best currants, one-half pound of butter, one pound of candied lemon peel, a scant half ounce of powdered allspice, one-half ounce of powdered cinnamon. Make a nice pastry, cut it into oblong or diamond shape, cut a little cross in the upper crust, fill and bake.—Mrs H. G. Taft.

Dried Apple Cake

Two cups of syrup or molasses, three cups of dried apples, one cup of butter, one cup of sugar, one cup of sour milk, one teaspoon of soda, four eggs, four cups of flour, one cup of currants (or more), one cup raisins (or more), one teaspoon cloves, one teaspoon cinnamon, one nutmeg, two teaspoons of yeast powder. Soak apples in as little water as possible over night; in the morning chop fine and boil one-half hour in molasses. When cold, add butter, sugar, and milk with soda dissolved, eggs, flour,

fruit, spices, and yeast powder.—Mrs
H. N. Stevens.

Ginger Wafers

Stir half a cup of butter to a cream.
Add gradually one cup of pulverized
sugar and one tablespoon of ginger. Add
half a cup of cold water and two cups
of sifted flour. Spread thin on a baking sheet and bake in a cool oven. Cut
into squares, triangles or cubes with a
sharp knife and remove from the baking
sheet by slipping a limber knife under
them. The baking sheet should be well
greased and quite cold when the dough
is spread on it.—Emma P. Ewing.

Chocolate Hearts

Melt, by standing over hot water,
three ounces of unsweetened chocolate;
add a pound of sifted powdered sugar
and mix thoroughly; work to a stiff yet
pliable paste with the unbeaten whites of
three eggs (or less), adding vanilla to
flavor. If the paste seems too soft add
more sugar. Break off in small pieces
and roll out about one-fourth of an inch
thick, sprinkling the board and paste
with granulated sugar instead of flour.
Cut with a tiny heart-shaped cake cutter
(any other small cake cutter will do),
and place on pans oiled just enough to
prevent sticking. Bake in a very moderate oven. When done, they will feel
firm to the touch, a solid crust having
formed over the top. They should be
very light, and will loosen easily from
the pan after being allowed to stand a
moment to cool. The success of these
cakes depends upon the oven, which
should be not as cool as for meringues,
not quite so hot as for sponge cake. If
properly made, they are very excellent
and but little labor. Use the yolks for
chocolate whips.—Amelia Sulzbacher.

Chocolate Cookies

Take a scant cup of butter, a heaping
cup of light brown sugar, two eggs, a
teaspoon of cinnamon, half a teaspoon

of cloves, a cup of almonds, cut fine, without blanching, a cup of currants, cleaned and dried, two ounces of unsweetened chocolate dissolved in half a cup of milk, and flour enough to roll; before adding the flour, put into it a heaping teaspoon of baking powder. Mix in the order given; roll out about one-eighth of an inch thick; cut with any preferred cake cutter and bake in a moderate oven. Make a rather thick syrup of half a cup each of granulated sugar and water boiled together, and brush the cakes with this syrup as soon as they are taken from the oven.—Amelia Sulzbacher.

Strawberry Eclairs

Boil together in a saucepan one cup of boiling water, one-fourth cup of butter and a speck of salt. As it begins to boil stir in one cup of sifted flour. Stir constantly until the mixture leaves the sides of the pan and cleaves together in a ball. When partly cool add four eggs, beating them in one at a time. Drop carefully in long narrow strips, some distance apart, on buttered tins, and bake in a moderate oven until well risen—about thirty minutes. Leave the oven door open a few minutes before removing the eclairs, to prevent their falling. When they are cool split one side, fill with sweetened strawberries or jam. Spread with boiled icing colored with strawberry juice.—Annabel Lee.

Chocolate Nougat Cake

One-half cup of sugar, one-half cup of sweet milk, one-half cake of chocolate and the yolks of two eggs. Cook this in a double boiler and cool. One and one-half cups of sugar, three eggs, one-half cup of butter, one-half cup of milk, two cups of flour, one teaspoon of soda dissolved in a little hot water. Add the cooled mixture last. Flavor with vanilla. This can be baked as a loaf or layer cake. Use the whites of the two eggs for frosting. For the layer cake

blanched almonds or walnuts should be thrown on the frosting between the layers and on the top. I prefer English walnuts. — Mrs George H. Russel, Detroit.

Cymbals

One cup of sugar, one-half cup of butter, two eggs, one-half cup of sour milk, one-half nutmeg, one teaspoon of saleratus. Stir butter and sugar together, add eggs and a little flour. Stir in the milk and saleratus, which should be previously strained. Add flour to make stiff enough to roll out. Cut into rings, sift sugar on top, and bake in a quick oven.—Mrs Benjamin M. Page, Pasadena.

Ladyfingers

Beat the whites of three eggs till dry, add one-third of a cup of powdered sugar gradually and continue beating. Then add the yolks, beaten till lemon-colored, and a quarter of a teaspoon of vanilla. Cut and fold in three-quarters of a cup of flour mixed with one-eighth teaspoon of salt. Shape with a pastry bag and tube on unbuttered sheets of paper. Sprinkle with powdered sugar and bake eight minutes in a moderate oven. Remove from the paper with a knife.—Stella A. Downing.

An Inexpensive Cake

One cup of black molasses, one-half cup of brown sugar, one-half cup of butter, one cup of hot water, one dessert-spoon of soda, two cups of flour, one dessertspoon of spices, using ginger or not, to your taste. This may be used for pudding, or by adding fruit makes a nice fruit cake. Bake in a quick oven.— Mary Miner.

Butter Sponge Cake

Two cups of sugar, one of butter, six eggs beaten separately, one-half cup of milk, one-half cup of water, two tea-spoons of baking powder, three cups of

flour. Mix butter and sugar to a cream. Add yolks. Do not beat much. Next milk, with whites and flour last. Bake in loaf or cup cakes.—Nettie C. Moore.

Celestial Cake

Bake an angel cake in a large round, shallow basin, when cold cut into wedge shaped pieces, reverse the pieces and put them together with points out, making it in form of a star. Cover with icing and garnish with bits of green angelica and red candied cherries.—Linda Hull Larned.

White Almond Cake

One-half cup butter, one and one-half cups sugar, one teaspoon almond extract, one-half cup milk, one and one-half cups pastry flour, one-half cup cornstarch and two teaspoons baking powder, stiffly beaten whites of five eggs. Sift together the flour, cornstarch and baking powder and add alternately with the milk. Mix in the order given and bake in a moderate oven.

Ice Cream Cake

Cream one cup of sugar with one-half cup of butter. Add one-half cup of milk, one and three-fourths cups of flour sifted with two level teaspoons of baking powder. Beat well and fold in the beaten whites of three eggs and add one-half teaspoon of vanilla. Bake in two round tins or one biscuit tin from twenty to thirty minutes. Frost with the yolks of two eggs, thickened with confectioner's sugar and flavored with vanilla. This same cake recipe, flavored with almond extract and frosted with a boiled icing containing one-half cup of chopped blanched almonds, makes a delicious almond cake.

Hot Water Sponge Cake

Beat the whites of three eggs, add one cup of fine sugar, then three yolks well beaten, one teaspoon of vanilla or lemon, one cup of pastry flour sifted with one-half teaspoon of baking powder, and

two tablespoons of boiling water. Bake in a loaf from twenty to thirty-five minutes.

Sponge Drops

Beat three eggs lightly, add three-fourths of a cup of granulated sugar, one heaping cup of flour sifted with one teaspoon of cream of tartar and one-half teaspoon of soda (or one heaping teaspoon of baking powder). Flavor with one teaspoon of lemon extract. Drop in teaspoons, three inches apart, on buttered tins. Bake in a quick oven. It is safe to bake one cake as a trial to see if the mixture needs any more flour. The cakes should spread in the oven, and they ought to be about one-half inch thick when baked.

Orange Sponge Cake

` Beat three eggs hard for five minutes. Then add one cup of granulated sugar and beat for three minutes. Add one-half cup of cold water, two cups of flour sifted with two teaspoons of baking powder. Bake in two deep jelly tins or in a biscuit tin from fifteen to twenty minutes. Thicken the unbeaten white of one egg with confectioner's sugar. Add the juice and grated peel of one-half an orange, and more sugar till the frosting is thick enough to spread on the cake. This cake is more tender and delicate the day after it is baked. Spread cut-up peaches or oranges between the layers and sprinkle powdered sugar over the top to make a dessert.—Annabel Lee.

Angel Cake

Beat the whites of eight eggs till frothy. Then add one teaspoon of cream of tartar and continue beating till the whites are perfectly stiff. Gradually add one cup of sugar, beating hard all the time. Sift together three-fourths of a cup of flour and one-fourth of a teaspoon of salt, and fold it lightly into the beaten whites. Flavor with three-fourths of a teaspoon of vanilla and pour into an

unbuttered angel cake pan. Put into a rather hot oven and allow the cake to rise quickly. Cool it off slightly, and as soon as the cake begins to brown cover with buttered paper. It will take from forty-five to fifty minutes to bake.

Gold Cake

Cream one-fourth cup of butter, add one-half cup of sugar slowly, and continue beating. Add the yolks of five eggs beaten until thick and lemon colored and one teaspoon of orange extract. Mix and sift seven-eighths cup of pastry flour with one and one-half teaspoons of baking powder, and add alternately with one-fourth cup of milk to the first mixture. Bake in a buttered and floured tin.— Stella A. Downing.

Chocolate Cake

One heaping tablespoon of butter, one cup of granulated sugar, yolks of three eggs, whites of four eggs, one teaspoon of cream tartar, one-half teaspoon of soda, one pinch of salt, one-half teaspoon of vanilla extract, one and one-half cups of flour, one-half cup of milk.

Filling : One-fourth cake of chocolate, two tablespoons of water and one heaping cup of powdered sugar.—Mrs Dan R. Hanna.

Devil's Food Cake

Two and a half cups of sifted flour, two cups of sugar, one-half cup of butter, one-half cup of sour milk, one-half cup of hot water, two eggs, one-half or one-fourth cake of chocolate, one teaspoon of vanilla, one teaspoon of soda. Grate chocolate and dissolve with the soda in the hot water. Use white icing. —Mrs Nelson Ruggles.

Boiled Icing

Boil one cup of granulated sugar with one-fourth cup of water, until the syrup hairs when dropped from a spoon. Have ready the beaten white of one egg. Pour the syrup slowly upon the egg, stirring

constantly. Flavor the same as the cake and spread on the cold cake, when the icing is stiff enough not to run. Cut in squares or slices.

Delicate Cake

Beat the yolks of five eggs till thick and lemon colored, stir in one cup of granulated sugar, the grated rind of one lemon and one tablespoon of the juice. Whip the whites of the eggs till quite stiff, add a few tablespoons of the froth to the beaten yolks, then one cup of pastry flour. Fold in the rest of the beaten whites. Bake as a loaf cake in a moderate oven, for nearly an hour. Cover with a soft boiled icing when the loaf has cooled, and before the icing dries, sprinkle with chopped almonds.— Mrs A. A. Lindeke.

Marguerites

Cut a sheet of sponge cake into small rounds, dip in confectioner's chocolate. While this is still moist lay split blanched almonds cut in halves around each little cake like the petals of the daisy. Into the center drop the daisy heart, made of fondant colored yellow. For a change you may use white fondant and split almonds which have been delicately browned in the oven, making the marguerite heart of chocolate.—See Page XXIX.

Cereals and Macaroni

Macaroni

Make strong beef broth the day before macaroni is to be served. Let it stand over night. In the morning it should be like a stiff jelly. Lift off the cake of cold fat from the top. Put one-half pound of macaroni into a large pan, over it pour absolutely boiling water, enough to cover it—to swim it. Let it boil continuously for half an hour. Into the broth put one can of strained tomatoes (so as to remove the seeds), two onions, one teaspoon of ground cloves, one teaspoon of ground allspice, one-half teaspoon of ground mace, three bay leaves, six dried mushrooms. Boil all this until it is a thick paste. Then pour the cooked and drained macaroni into a large hot plate.

Honeycomb Timbale

Boil, in salted water, large-sized macaroni. When cold, cut it into pieces one-quarter of an inch long, making rings. Butter a plain, dome-shaped quart mold and cover it with the rings Make a sauce of one tablespoon each of butter and flour, half a cup each of stock and milk, one-half a teaspoon of salt and a little pepper. Mix with minced chicken or turkey and stir over the fire till the meat is heated. Remove from the range, add three beaten eggs and turn into the lined mold and cover it with a greased paper. Place it in a pan of hot water and poach in a slow oven twenty minutes. Unmold onto a round dish, garnish with cress and a ring of sauted mushrooms.

Mush

The water must be fresh, fiercely boiling; and *all* the meal, as it is deftly sprinkled in, must encounter the same high temperature, that the starch cells

may burst. Have a large, porcelain-lined iron pot and a wooden paddle for stirring. Stir with one hand while sprinkling in the meal with the other. The proportions will vary with the degree of "flouriness" of the meal, and its coarseness, but an average rule would be four quarts of water, one of meal and two tablespoons of salt. When the meal is all in the pot should be closely covered and stood where it will only give an occasional bubble, for three or four hours, or even half a day. Do not disturb the surface, thus permitting the extractives (flavors) to escape.

Fried Mush

Make as above and pour into tins with straight sides, as bread pans. When cold cut into half-inch slices and fry in deep fat, or saute ("pan-fry") in a spider in fat a quarter of an inch deep. Be sure the fat is sweet and that it is hot when the mush is put in, that there may be no grease soaking. Fry to a rich even brown.—Ella Morris Kretschmar.

Cheese

Cheese Balls for Salad

To two packages of Neufchatel cheese add one-half teaspoon of onion juice and two tablespoons of lemon juice. Add a dash of ground tabasco if desired. Mold into small balls with butter paddles and serve with lettuce or salad.—Lida P. Wilson, Omaha.

Cheese Balls Fried

Mix thoroughly a cup and a half of grated cheese, a little salt and pepper and the whites of three eggs, beaten stiff. Shape into little rolls, cover with bread *dust,* fry in deep fat and drain on blotting paper.—Anne Warner.

Cottage Cheese

Place a panful of clabbered milk over a pan of hot water. Let it heat slowly till the curd separates; do not allow to boil or it will be tough. Strain through a cloth bag and press out all the whey; stir in a little butter and salt, and as much thick sweet cream as possible and still have it retain its form when turned from a mold or rolled into balls. Work it well with a spoon until it becomes fine-grained.—Anne Warner.

Cheese Ramekin

Put one cup of bread crumbs and one gill of milk on the fire to boil. Stir and boil until smooth. Then put in four tablespoons of grated cheese, a little piece of butter, and salt and pepper. Stir till the cheese is dissolved, then remove from the fire. Beat two eggs, the yolks and whites separately. Stir the yolks into the mixture and then the whites of the eggs. Put in a pudding dish and bake fifteen or twenty minutes.—Mrs W. G. Trowbridge.

A Really Digestible Welsh Rarebit

Melt one tablespoon of butter, add one-fourth of a teaspoon of salt and paprika, half a teaspoon of dry mustard and one-third of a cup of ale or beer. Stir constantly, and when hot put in half a pound of cheese cut into small pieces. As it gradually melts it may thicken, for no cheese is exactly alike in the amount of liquid it requires. If it seems too thick, add more beer. If the rarebit is preferred creamy instead of stringy, add one beaten egg just before serving. The paprika in this recipe makes the cheese mixture perfectly digestible. If the regulation toast is not at hand for serving rarebit, pour it over saltines.— I. G. C.

Escalloped Cheese

Butter a baking dish, put in a layer of bread cut into inch squares, add a layer of cheese cut small, dust with salt and paprika. Add more bread, about one-half a stale loaf, and one cup of cheese, and one-half teaspoon of salt. Beat two eggs light, add one pint of milk and pour over the bread and cheese. Bake for one-half hour in a moderate oven.

Mrs Mac's Cheese

One-quarter pound of well-ripened Roquefort cheese grated; add one tablespoon of butter, one also of brandy, one-half saltspoon of salt, dash of tabasco, a little paprika. Mix thoroughly till pasty and put in small jars or cups. When hard turn out and serve with coffee. The longer it stands the better it is.—Mrs McLaren.

Cold Desserts

Chocolate Whips

Beat the yolks of three eggs and three tablespoons of sugar until light. Dissolve one heaping tablespoon of grated unsweetened chocolate, one tablespoon of sugar and one tablespoon of hot water; when dissolved, add slowly a pint of milk heated to boiling; pour this hot mixture over the beaten eggs and sugar, and cook in a double boiler, stirring constantly until it thickens. When cool flavor with vanilla and place on the ice. When ready to serve half fill small punch glasses with the custard and heap cream whipped, sweetened and flavored over it.—Amelia Sulzbacher.

Jerusalem Pudding

Boil a quarter of a cup of rice twenty minutes, drain and throw into a bowl of cold water. Cut three figs and three ounces of preserved ginger into tiny pieces, cover with a gill of sherry and soak fifteen minutes. Cover half a box of gelatine with half a cup of cold water and soak thirty minutes. Whip one pint of cream, put into a basin and stand on the ice or in a very cold place. Sprinkle over the cream half a cup of powdered sugar and a scant teaspoon of vanilla. Drain the rice and spread it on a towel to dry, after which add it to the cream, stirring lightly; then add fruit, and lastly the dissolved gelatine, and stir into the mixture. Stir all slowly until it begins to harden, and then turn it into a mold that has been filled with water. Do not wipe the mold.—Mrs Clinton Locke, Chicago.

Heavenly Hash

Select twelve medium-sized oranges of good shape and color. Cut a small circular piece from the stem end of each and remove the pulp in small pieces with

a spoon.   To the pulp add one small can of pineapple (sliced), two ripe bananas, quartered and sliced, one-quarter pound of seeded Malaga grapes.   Sweeten to taste.   Fill the orange shells and garnish with candied cherries.—Miss Nellie Taylor, Rockford.

Banana Pudding

One box of gelatine, one pint of cream, one quart of milk, two cups of sugar, five bananas.   Dissolve gelatine in a cup of water, add sugar to the milk and let it scald, take some of the hot milk and thin the gelatine, strain and let it simmer ten minutes, pour in a bowl to cool.   Peel bananas and break in small pieces with a fork and stir into the mixture, when cool but not stiff.   Serve with whipped cream on top flavored with vanilla.—Mrs Charles Sherlock.

Compote of Marshmallows

Preserved peaches (fresh fruit is better if in season), Maraschino cherries, oranges, pecan nuts, and fresh marshmallows.   Cut in halves and then quarter the peaches and oranges.   Mix in the nuts and marshmallows with the fruit juice.   Cover all with whipped cream and garnish the top with the cherries. Serve cold.—Mrs Clarence W. Cady

Wigwam Pudding

One-fourth pound of ladyfingers, one pint of milk, a teaspoon of vanilla, one gill of sherry, one tumbler of jelly or jam, four eggs, eight tablespoons of powdered sugar.   Split the ladyfingers and spread the flat side with the jelly; dip the crust side in the sherry.   Line the bottom and sides of the dish in which you wish to serve it with those ladyfingers, log cabin style, in the center of the dish—that is, cross them so that the custard will pass between.   Now put the milk to heat in double boiler.   Beat the yolks of eggs, and stir together with one-half the sugar until light, add to milk and stir until it thickens ; add the

vanilla and stand aside to cool. Beat the whites of the eggs, adding the sugar gradually till thick and frothy; add lemon. Pour the custard over the ladyfingers, heap the meringue over the top and stand on a board in the oven to brown. Brown quickly before the dish heats or the custard will curdle.—Mrs A. J. Aikens.

Pineapple Sponge

One small fresh pineapple or a pint and a half can of the fruit, one small cup of sugar, half a package of granulated gelatine, one cup and a half of water, the whites of four eggs. Soak the gelatine in a half cup of water, until dissolved. Chop the pineapple, and put it, together with the juice, in a saucepan with the sugar and remainder of the water. Simmer ten minutes, add the gelatine, take from fire immediately, and strain into a basin. When partially cooled, add the whites of the eggs and heat until the mixture begins to thicken. Pour into a mold, and set it away to harden. Serve with soft custard.—Mrs William Lansing.

Macaroon Cream

Soak one tablespoon of granulated gelatine in one-fourth cup of cold water. Make a custard of two cups of scalded milk, yolks of three eggs, one-third cup of sugar, one-eighth teaspoon of salt; add the soaked gelatine. When dissolved, strain, cool, add two-thirds cup of pounded macaroons, one teaspoon vanilla, stirring until the mixture begins to thicken, then add the whites beaten until stiff and dry. Mold, chill and serve with a garnish of whipped cream.

Apple Porcupine

Make a syrup by boiling eight minutes one and one-half cups of sugar and one and one-half cups of water. Wipe, pare and core eight apples. Put apples in syrup as soon as pared so they won't discolor. Cook until soft, occasionally

skimming the syrup during cooking.
Apples cook better covered with the
syrup; therefore it is better to use a deep
saucepan and have two cookings. Drain
apple from syrup; cool, fill cavities with
jelly, marmalade or preserved fruit, and
stick the apples with almonds blanched
and split in halves lengthwise. Serve
with cream sauce.—Mrs Chester Sim-
mons.

Salpicon of Fruit

This is served in glass punch or
custard cups. In the bottom of each put
a slice of orange, on this lay one-half of
a fine white peach (if brandied, all the
better); the top layer should be of
Maraschino cherries and the cups filled
two-thirds full of a mixture of liquid
from the cherries and a small quantity
of orange juice; if this is not sufficient
add a little strained liquor from the can
of peaches. Set the cups, covered, in a
shallow pan of cracked ice and a sprinkling of salt, till needed.

French Strawberries

Fill punch cups one-third full of very
ripe red berries, sliced; add a tablespoon
of granulated sugar to each cup and fill
three-quarters full with strained orange
juice. Stir gently to dissolve sugar and
set the cups into a pan of cracked ice
till served. When these simple ingredients are first put together the combination of color is really dreadful to con-
template, so give the mixture at least
three hours to ripen and beautify. Val-
encia oranges are the most satisfactory
for this use in strawberry time.

Glorified Rice

Soak half a box of gelatine in half a
cup of cold water. Wash half a cup of
rice and sprinkle into boiling salted
water. Boil till tender and dry thoroughly in a napkin. Dissolve the gelatine over hot water and cool. Whip one
pint of rich cream, fold into it the gelatine, the cold rice, half a cup of powdered

sugar and a teaspoon of vanilla. Pour
into a mold. When ready to serve turn
out of the mold and pour over it the
following sauce: One-half tumbler of
quince jelly melted over the fire with
three tablespoons of cold water.—Mrs
W. Austin Goodman.

Porcupine Pudding and Caramel Sauce

This is merely a development of the
caramel custard of our foremothers, but
it always reflects credit upon the hostess.
Melt one cup of granulated sugar and
one tablespoon of water in a saucepan.
Stir only long enough to melt, then let
it cook till it becomes a light brown
color. Add one cup of boiling water
and stand on the side of the range till
the caramel is dissolved. Reserve half
of this to pour round the pudding. Stir
the remainder, with a half teaspoon of
vanilla and a pinch of salt, into a pint
of hot milk. Pour this over two whole
eggs and four yolks slightly beaten.
Strain into a shallow flat mold or pan,
so that the custard is not over two inches
deep. Place the mold in a pan of hot
water and bake in a very slow oven until
firm in the center; test by running in a
knife. It should take thirty or forty
minutes and will be firm and smooth.
Serve very cold, unmolding onto a flat
white and gold dish, with an edge only
deep enough to hold the clear golden-
brown sauce as it spreads. The entire
top surface of the pudding should be
thickly studded with spikes made of
almonds, which have been blanched, cut
in shreds and browned slightly in the
oven.—Anne Warner.

Rhubarb Jelly

Skin and cut one pound of rhubarb in
small pieces. Put into a saucepan with
one cup of sugar and a small piece of
fresh ginger root and cook slowly until
soft, but not broken. Soak two tablespoons of granulated gelatine in one-half
cup of cold water until soft, then strain
into the hot rhubarb, with two table-

spoons of lemon juice. Mold, chill and
serve with a garnish of whipped cream.

Rhubarb with Figs

Wash half a pound of bag or pulled
figs and cook in boiling water to cover
until the water is nearly absorbed. Skin
and cut a pound of rhubarb in one-inch
pieces. Put a layer in a baking dish,
sprinkle with sugar, add a layer of figs,
repeat until all is used; put in one-
fourth cup of hot water and bake in a
slow oven until the rhubarb is soft.
Dates or raisins may be used in the same
manner.

Almond Charlotte

Three-fourths cup of fine sugar, one-
fourth cup of butter, whites of three
eggs, one cup of flour, one level teaspoon
baking powder, one-fourth cup of milk;
flavor with almond and bake delicately
in a square layer tin. Whip one pint of
cream, sweetened and slightly flavored
with almond, until very stiff. Pile thick
on the cake and sprinkle thick with
almonds, blanched and cut into shreds.—
Mrs Robert Russell.

Pineapple Bavarian Cream

Soak one-half box or two tablespoons
of granulated gelatine in one-half cup of
cold water. Heat one can grated pineapple, add one-half cup sugar, one tablespoon lemon juice and the soaked gelatine. Stir until the gelatine is dissolved,
then chill in a pan of ice water, stirring
constantly; when it begins to thicken,
fold in the whip from three cups of
cream. Mold and chill. Serve with
cubes of lemon jelly.

Whipped Peach Cream in Baskets

Beat the whites of four eggs until
very stiff, then mix in by degrees four
level tablespoons of powdered sugar,
next add two tablespoons of rich peach
syrup (drained from preserved peaches),
and stir in lightly one pint of sweet
cream. Whisk to a stiff froth. Every-

thing should be very cold before beginning, and keep the bowl containing the cream in a pan of cracked ice while whipping the ingredients. Have ready round individual sponge cakes, scoop out the center until the walls and bottom are only three-fourths of an inch thick, and just before serving fill with the peach cream. If an especially handsome dessert is wanted, brush the outside of the basket with white of egg, and stick all over it halved English walnut meats or pecans.

Peach Delight

Pare, cut in halves and stone a dozen fine ripe peaches, reserving a few of the pits. Boil the pits in half a cup of water for fifteen minutes, then strain. Mix well together a generous half cup of sugar and a tablespoon of flour. Butter a deep pudding dish well, put in a layer of peaches, sprinkle with the sugar, dot with bits of butter, cover with another layer of the peaches and proceed in this way until all are used. Pour over the water which was strained off the pits. Make a rich biscuit crust for the top, roll out about half an inch thick, place it over the fruit, make several incisions to allow the steam to escape, and bake in a moderate oven. In serving, cut the crust in pieces as for pie, put the fruit on top and cover with whipped or plain cream.

Pineapple Tapioca

Four tablespoons of pearl tapioca, one pint of shredded preserved pineapple. Simmer the tapioca until clear but not entirely dissolved. Stir the pineapple in tapioca. If not sweet enough add sugar. Serve with clear or whipped cream. A very simple and dainty dessert.—Mrs Homer T. Yaryan.

Norwegian Prune Pudding

One pound of prunes, one quart of water, two cups of sugar, five tablespoons of cornstarch, a small piece of stick cinnamon. Soak the prunes in cold water

over night, and boil in the same water.
Stone, add one pint of water, put on to
cook again, and while boiling, add
sugar, cinnamon and cornstarch mixed
with a little cold water. Boil five minutes, stirring occasionally. Pour in a
mold to cool.—Mrs William Christie
Herron.

Stewed California Prunes or Figs (Black)

Wash the figs or prunes well in two
waters, put in a saucepan and completely cover with water (preferably
distilled). Stew gently until nearly all
the water is absorbed and the fruit is
plump. Do not use any sugar. Cooked
in this way the flavor is preserved, and
the fruit is very nourishing. I never
soak prunes.

California Prunes Stewed with Muscatel Grapes

Prunes cooked in this way are delicious. It takes a little time to prepare
them, but is worth the trouble. Take
two pounds of ripe Muscatel grapes,
wash, strip from the bunches into a
saucepan, add a very little water (distilled) and stew gently until tender,
crushing the grapes to extract all the
flavor and juice, then strain. Wash a
pound of prunes, cover with the grape
juice and stew until the prunes absorb
most of the juice. Or the prunes and
grapes can be stewed together, the
grapes crushed and the seeds skimmed
off as they rise to the top.

Fruit Fillip

Cut four large oranges in two and
lift out carefully with an orange spoon
the sections of fruit. Free the inside of
each orange shell from skin and prepare
the following fruit salad: The pulp of
the oranges, kept as whole as possible,
two bananas cut in fine dice, three tablespoons of brandied cherries cut in halves,
half a cup of Malaga grapes, halved and
seeded, four tablespoons of powdered

sugar; over these pour two tablespoons of sherry and one teaspoon of rum. Allow this to stand on the ice half an hour, then fill each half of the orange with fillip. Serve on green leaves arranged on small plates.

Lemon Jelly

To one cup of sugar add a pint of water and allow it to boil twenty minutes. Before making the syrup, put two tablespoons of granulated gelatine to soak in half a cup of cold water. Pour over it the boiling syrup, add half a cup of lemon juice and the grated rind of one lemon. Strain through fine cheesecloth into a wet mold and allow it to set.

Compote of Greengages

Boil six ounces of sugar and one pint of water together for one-quarter of an hour. Skim well, put in one and one-half pounds of greengages, and simmer very gently for fifteen or twenty minutes, taking care the greengages do not break. When done let them cool a little, put them in a glass dish and pour the syrup over them.

Danish Pudding

Eight eggs beaten into three tablespoons of sugar; stir this into one quart of boiling cream, or milk if you can do no better. Melt in an ordinary spider one-third of a pound of brown sugar till it is a syrup, stirring all the time. Pour this into a pudding dish, which should be placed in a dripping pan of hot water, then pour the custard on top of syrup, and bake in the oven until the custard is firm. Turn out on dish just before serving, and a fine addition is to cover with whipped cream, though this is not necessary.— Irene W. Chittenden, Detroit.

Chocolate Pudding

To a quart of milk, allow a pint of fine bread, slices of bread or their equivalent in small pieces; crusts and "heels" may be used. Add three eggs, one small cup

of sugar, and two squares of chocolate melted, or three heaping teaspoons of cocoa, stirred dry with the sugar. Beat all together well and flavor with one teaspoon of vanilla, or one-half teaspoon of ground cinnamon, and half a teaspoon of salt. Bake in a buttered dish. Excellent hot or cold, and requires no sauce. Baked in custard cups and served cold with whipped cream, this is delicious.

Plums in Ambush

Boil rice in milk until tender and quite dry; sweeten it to taste with powdered sugar. Pour it into a border mold to set; if a border mold is not at hand, take one of the ordinary kind of a plain pattern; set a jam pot nearly filled with water in the center, then pour the rice into the mold and set away to get cold. When ready to serve, remove the jar, turn the rice out carefully (it should form a compact wall), and fill the hollow with rich stewed plums. Pour a little of the syrup over the rice, and mask the plums with whipped cream.

Plum Trifle

Cut damson plums in half, and cook until tender in a little syrup; drain, and rub the pulp through a coarse sieve. To a cup of the pulp when cold add the stiffly whipped whites of four eggs. Fill glass custard cups half full of vanilla custard, and when very cold, put a large spoon of the trifle on top, heaping it up roughly. Serve very cold.—Mary Foster Snider.

Plum Shape

Put one-half pound of fine ripe plums into an enameled saucepan, pour over them one cup of sugar and one cup of water, and simmer gently until they are quite soft. Remove the stones, and drain off the syrup. Put the pulp into a bowl, return the syrup to the saucepan, and dissolve in it one-half ounce of gelatine which has been softened in a little cold water. If not sweet enough, add more

sugar, then add the plum pulp, and one-half cup of blanched almonds coarsely chopped. Mix all well together, pour the mixture into a border mold, and stand aside to set. When quite cold, turn out onto a glass dish, and fill up the center with whipped cream. Stick blanched almonds cut in strips all over the jelly.

Prunes in Jelly

Soak two heaping dessertspoons of granulated gelatine in one cup of cold water for one hour. Add one cup of boiling water, one cup of sugar, one cup of white wine or sherry and the juice of one lemon. Cut twelve cooked prunes in quarters. Have ready a mold wet in cold water. Strain into it enough jelly to give about one inch in thickness. Let this harden, add the prunes at equal distances apart, then a second layer of jelly, and when that has hardened, repeat the layers till the mold is filled. When hard, turn out the jelly and serve with whipped cream.

Plum Salad

Into a glass salad bowl put one-half pint each of greengages, stoned and cut in half, bananas, peeled and cut in slices, and any other fresh fruit that is at hand. Sprinkle well with powdered sugar, cover and let stand one hour, then add one wineglass of syrup of preserved cherries, one of lemon juice, and the greengage kernels, blanched and cut in half. Cover again and let stand until required. Serve with whipped cream and sponge fingers. The cream and fingers should not be put on the salad, but should be served separately.

Plums in Jelly

Soak two ounces of gelatine in a pint and a half of water for one hour; then add the juice of three lemons, one-half pound of loaf sugar, and the whites of five eggs beaten in a gill of water. Stir all together over the fire until boiling.

Then pass through a flannel jelly bag
several times, until quite clear. Cut two
dozen ripe plums into strips, take the
kernels out of the stones, and mix both
fruit and kernels in the jelly. Pour it
into a wet mold, and set aside until firm.
When required to serve, turn out on a
glass or silver dish. Serve with whipped
cream and macaroons.

Jellied Prune Ring

Soak one-third of a pound of prunes
over night in cold water. In the morning simmer slowly till soft. Stone them
and cut in pieces. To the prune juice
add enough boiling water to make two
cups of liquid, pour it over two and one-
half tablespoons of gelatine dissolved in
half a cup of water, then add one
cup of sugar and four tablespoons of
lemon juice. Strain, add the cut prunes
and pour into a ring mold. Turn out
when thoroughly chilled. Fill the center
with whipped cream sweetened and flavored with vanilla. Garnish the base
of the dish with well plumped cooked
prunes and whipped cream squeezed
through a pastry tube.—See Page XX.

Eggs

Savory Stuffed Eggs in Mayonnaise

Cut twelve hard-boiled eggs into halves lengthwise. Take out the yolks, put them through a potato ricer and mix them with two tablespoons each of melted butter, anchovy paste and chopped ham. Add half a teaspoon of paprika. Press this egg paste into each white and lay them together. When ready to serve pour over the dish a tumbler of mayonnaise.

My Favorite Omelet

Six eggs, one tablespoon of butter, one tablespoon of flour, one cup of cold milk, one-half teaspoon of salt. Put the butter in a granite saucepan, and when it is melted (but not cooked hard), add the flour. Mix well. Now add the cold milk all at once, and stir until smooth. Set aside to cool. Add the salt. Then separate the eggs, beating yolks until very light and whites until very stiff. Fold first the yolks and then the whites into the sauce very carefully. Then put all into a granite baking dish and bake in moderate oven fifteen or twenty minutes. Serve immediately in the dish in which it was baked.—Mrs Grace E. Dutton, Pasadena.

Orange Omelet, with Whipped Cream

Three eggs, two tablespoons of powdered sugar, a few grains of salt, one teaspoon of lemon juice, two oranges, one-half tablespoon of butter, two and one-half tablespoons of orange juice; separate yolks from whites, beat yolks until thick and lemon colored, add seasonings, fold in whites beaten to a foam, cook in smooth frying pan or omelet pan in the hot butter, cook slowly, turning the pan that the omelet may brown evenly; when delicately browned underneath, place on

the center or upper grate of the oven to cook or dry the top, fold, turn on hot platter, sprinkle with powdered sugar, garnish with slices of orange, serve with stiffly beaten whipped cream.

Omelet Souffle

One cup of flour, one pint of milk, one tablespoon of sugar, butter size of a walnut. Scald milk, flour and butter. After the batter is cold stir in yolks of five eggs. Add beaten whites just before baking. Bake in a quick oven and serve with hard sauce.—Mrs Antes Ruhl, Rockford, Ill.

Scotch Eggs

Cook six eggs hard and at the same time keep them tender by leaving in hot water just below the boiling point for one-half hour; cool and remove the shells. Cook to a paste one-third of a cup of bread crumbs in one-third of a cup of milk and add one cup of deviled ham and one raw egg. Cover the eggs with the mixture, roll in crumbs and fry brown in hot fat. Cut in halves lengthwise and send to the table on a bed of parsley and garnish with bacon cooked in the manner given below: slice as thin as possible. Hold the bacon, rind down, and do not try to cut through it till you have the required number of slices, then shave it all at one time from the rind. Separate the slices and lay on a fine wire broiler, put over a pan and place in a hot oven till the bacon is transparent. Do not burn it.—Anne Warner.

Omelet with Tomato Sauce

Four eggs, four tablespoons cold water, two tablespoons butter and one of flour, salt and paprika to taste. Beat eggs thoroughly—yolks until thick and lemon colored, whites until stiff and dry. To the beaten yolks add flour and seasoning, then the water; lastly fold in the whites, taking care not to beat, as that will make the omelet tough. Have the butter hot, but not browned, in an

omelet pan, pour in the mixture, with a spatula lift gently from the center until it is set, then place the pan in a moderate oven a few minutes to slightly brown the top. While this is being done, make sauce by blending together the butter and flour, adding the cup of strained tomato, onion juice and seasoning. Cook until the mixture thickens. If eggs are perfectly fresh and well beaten, the omelet may be too thick to fold. If so, slip off on to hot chop plate, and pour the sauce around it. If not, fold over gently, garnish with the sauce and serve at once on hot plates. If the tomato sauce is not liked, sprinkle and garnish with chopped parsley, with minced ham, or jelly, as preferred. When carefully made this is one of the daintiest of breakfast dishes.—Mary Moody Pugh, Omaha.

Creamed Eggs for Luncheon

One-half dozen hard boiled eggs cut in halves. Make a white sauce as follows: Two teaspoons of butter, two level tablespoons of flour; melt butter and stir in flour, then add slowly one-half pint of milk, seasoning with salt and pepper and a little celery if desired. Pour over eggs and serve in dish garnished with parsley.—Mrs Scot Butler.

Snow Omelet

Beat the yolks of four eggs, add four tablespoons of milk or water, a little salt and pepper. Beat the whites very light and cut them into the yolks. Melt one dessertspoon of butter in a frying pan; when it bubbles, pour in the omelet and spread it evenly over the pan. When slightly brown underneath, sprinkle over the surface one tablespoon of grated cheese, chopped ham or parsley, place the pan in the oven to dry the omelet a moment, turn onto a hot platter and serve at once.

Scrambled Eggs

Beat five eggs till slightly blended, add a dust of white pepper, half a tea-

spoon of salt and half a cup of milk.
Melt two tablespoons of butter in the
chafing-dish, pour in the egg mixture
and cook till it is creamy, scraping it
from the bottom of the pan as it becomes thick.   Scrambled eggs are nice
accompanied by saltine wafers.   A
delicious variation is to butter slices of
bread, spread thinly with anchovy paste
and then cover with scrambled egg.   A
cheese flavor may be added by mixing
just before serving with a quarter of a
cup of grated cheese and a generous
dust of paprika.

Egg Timbale

Six eggs beaten slightly, one level
teaspoon of salt, one shake of pepper for
each egg, one-half pepperspoon of red
pepper, one and one-quarter cups of
milk, a little onion juice.   Put in small
cups in dipper and pour boiling water
around.   Bake from five to seven minutes in hot oven.   Turn into shallow
dish.

Sauce: One-half can of tomatoes, four
saltspoons of mixed pickle spice, one
bunch of thyme, one block of sugar
(loaf), one-half teaspoon of salt.   Let
cook until pulp of tomato is soft and
will pour through a sieve.   To this add
one heaping tablespoon of flour and cook
two minutes in a tablespoon of butter
and a little lemon juice.—Mrs Edgar E.
Bartlett, Rockford.

Fish

Fish Mousselines

Mince enough uncooked white fish to make two cups, add one cup of soft bread crumbs and one-half cup of cream. Press through a colander, season with salt, pepper, lemon juice, a suspicion of mace and Worcestershire sauce. Fold in carefully the beaten whites of four eggs. Turn into buttered molds (round bottomed ones) and steam one-half hour. Turn out on separate plates, surround with the sauce and drop tiny balls of boiled potato in the sauce. For sauce, make a stock of the fish bones and add it to two tablespoons of butter and two of flour cooked together. There should be one and one-half cups of stock. Add one-half cup of cream and when boiling add salt, pepper, and one tablespoon of grated horse-radish soaked in lemon juice.

Finnan Haddie

Braise two cups of finnan haddie that has been picked up fine in a lump of butter the size of a walnut, over the open fire. Add one cup of cream into which one tablespoon of flour has been rubbed smooth. Let come to a boil, and when cooled a little, add one large tablespoon of grated cheese, a trifle of pepper and, just before serving, the well beaten yolk of an egg. Serve on toast.—Mrs Edward Cahill.

Salmon Loaf

Take one can of salmon, drain off the juice, chop fine. Add yolks of four eggs beaten very light, one-half cup of grated bread crumbs, four tablespoons of melted butter, one-half teaspoon of pepper (scant), one-half teaspoon of salt, and a little finely chopped parsley. Beat whites of eggs stiff and add last. Put in buttered pan and bake half an hour.

Dressing for Loaf

One cup of sweet milk (added to the juice of the salmon), one tablespoon of butter, one tablespoon of flour. Cook until thick, add one egg beaten light. Pour over loaf.—Mrs W. H. Parsons.

Picked-up Codfish

Take two pounds of Nantucket codfish, cover it with cold water and soak over night. Then remove all bones and skin, shred into small pieces, cover with cold water, and place over the fire. As soon as it boils, pour off the water, taste of the fish, and if too salt, repeat the process. Once more drain off all the water and cover the fish with a cup and a half of rich milk, and let it cook slowly fifteen minutes. Add butter the size of a walnut, stir in quickly two eggs, remove from the fire, and serve at once.

Boiled Fish

Dredge the prepared fish with flour. Wrap in a cloth. Put in a steamer or in boiling water. When done, take from the kettle, drain, place upon a hot platter, remove the cloth, garnish with lemon points and sprigs of parsley and serve with drawn butter egg sauce. A medium-sized fish will boil in half an hour, and when sufficiently cooked will flake and separate easily.—Emma P. Ewing.

To Broil Salmon

Take two slices of salmon cut from the middle of the fish, sprinkle over a little lemon juice, cayenne pepper, salt and salad oil. Let it then remain for half an hour. Rub the gridiron well with beef suet or pork. As it is a nice matter to broil salmon without burning, it would be well to wrap it in buttered or oiled paper just before broiling. Serve with a maitre d'hotel, pickle, caper, anchovy or horse-radish sauce.

Sardine Rarebit

Broil the sardines. Toast some narrow strips of bread on one side and place the

sardines on the untoasted side. Set in the oven until the sauce is made. For every twenty sardines use the following ingredients: Melt one tablespoon of butter, add two tablespoons of grated cheese, stir until the cheese is melted and add gradually the beaten yolk of an egg mixed with one-fourth of a cup of thin cream. Stir until smooth and thickened; add half a teaspoon of salt, a teaspoon of tabasco sauce, and pour over the sardines, a few spoonfuls to each sardine. Serve at once with quarters of lemon.

Halibut in Cucumbers

Cook the halibut till tender, in court bouillon—to two quarts of water add a few slices each of carrot, onion and celery; two or three cloves and peppercorns; a bit each of mace, bay leaf and parsley, a little salt and lemon juice. Drain, and when cool remove skin and bone and pick the fish apart into fine flakes. Make a rich white sauce in the regular way, adding from a quarter to a half teaspoon of curry powder to every two cups of sauce, according to taste. Pare, cut in halves and parboil in bouillon the required number of cucumbers. Scoop out the inside of each half, fill with the creamed fish, cover with prepared crumbs—one-third cup of butter to every cup of dried bread crumbs— and bake about half an hour or less, till the cucumbers are soft, but not till they lose shape. Serve with a lemon point on each plate.—Anne Warner.

Filled Fish

Prepare trout, pickerel or pike in the following manner: After the fish has been scaled and thoroughly cleaned, remove all the meat that adheres to the skin, being careful not to injure the skin; take out all the meat from head to tail, cut open along the backbone, removing it also; but do not disfigure the head and tail. Still another way is to pull off the whole skin of the fish, then remove all the meat, being very careful not to have

any bones mixed with it; chop the meat in a chopping bowl, then heat about a quarter of a pound of butter in a spider, throw a handful of chopped parsley, and some soaked white bread; remove from the fire and add an onion grated, salt, pepper, pounded almond, three whole eggs and the yolks of two, also a very little nutmeg grated. Mix all thoroughly and fill the skin until it looks natural. Boil in salt water, containing a piece of butter, celery root and parsley and an onion; when done remove from the fire and lay on a platter. Have some almonds blanched, cut each almond lengthwise into four strips and stick them into the body of the fish. Thicken the fish sauce with yolks of eggs, adding a few slices of lemon.

Salmon Croquettes

Flake two cups of cold boiled or canned salmon with a silver fork. Season it with a little salt, mustard and cayenne. Mix with it one cup of thick cream sauce, made by blending together one tablespoon of butter with two tablespoons of flour, and adding gradually one cup of hot rich milk or thin cream. Cook this in a double boiler or saucepan until smooth and thick, seasoning the sauce with salt, pepper and celery salt. Spread the salmon mixture on a buttered platter to cool. Heat one cup of canned peas with three teaspoons of butter, one teaspoon of sugar, two teaspoons of flour and three tablespoons of thin cream. When the salmon is cold, shape a portion into a flat round cake, put a spoon of creamed peas in the center, cover with the salmon, make into a ball, dip in crumbs, beaten egg, and crumbs again, and fry to a golden brown in hot fat. Garnish with parsley.—Annabel Lee.

Salmon on Toast

Make a cup of drawn butter sauce by melting one tablespoon of butter, and stirring into it an even tablespoon of flour. When this is quite smooth, add

one cup of boiling milk. Season with
salt and cayenne pepper, or according to
taste, and stir in one large cup of salmon, picked into flakes. When quite hot,
add one egg, well beaten with three tablespoons of cold sweet cream. It should
be served smoking hot, poured over
round pieces of bread fried in butter. If
this is too rich, it is very good served
on toasted bread instead.—Mrs S. M.
Jones, Toledo, O.

Slices of Salmon Boiled

If a family is small and it should not
be advisable to buy a large middle cut
of salmon, it would be preferable to buy,
for instance, two slices. Boil them very
slowly in acidulated salted water, or in
the court bouillon, with wine. Serve
them with parsley between, and a napkin
underneath. Serve a sauce Hollandaise
in the sauce boat.

Fried Slices of Fish with Tomato Sauce

Bone and slice the fish, and cut it into
even slices; or if a flounder or any flat
fish is used, begin at the tail and, keeping
the knife close to the bone, separate each
side of the fish neatly from it, then cut
each side in two lengthwise, leaving the
fish in four long pieces. Remove the
skin carefully. After having sprinkled
pepper and salt over them, roll each piece
first in sifted cracker or bread crumbs,
then in half a cup of milk mixed with
an egg, and then in the crumbs again.
They are better fried in a saute pan in a
little hot butter; yet they may be sauted
in a little hot lard, with some neat slices
of pork, or fried in boiling lard. Pour
tomato sauce on a hot platter, arrange
the pieces of fish symmetrically on it,
and serve immediately.

Scalloped Fish

Use what is left from the baked or
boiled fish served at dinner. Remove the
bones and skin, break in pieces, mix with
it the dressing and sauce, if any. Arrange in a baking dish with alternate

layers of cracker crumbs, using butter,
pepper and salt, as needed. Have
crumbs come to the top, and moisten with
milk, using less if there is sauce. Bake
until brown and serve at once for luncheon or supper.

Codfish with Vegetables

Freshen codfish and cut it in chops
about three by six inches in size. Put
into hot water and set on the stove
where it will barely simmer. Boiling
hardens the fiber of fish as it does of
meat. When the fish is perfectly tender,
drain, pour over it a butter sauce and
serve for dinner with mashed potatoes,
beet pickles and boiled carrots.

Salmon Salad Molds

Mix two cups of cold boiled salmon,
one tablespoon of lemon juice, one teaspoon of chopped parsley, two drops of
tabasco sauce, one tablespoon of granulated gelatine dissolved in a little water
with enough cooked salad dressing to
moisten. Fill small molds, place on ice
for two or three hours, turn out on
lettuce leaves and serve with cucumber
cream sauce.—Stella A. Downing.

Salmon Turbot

Flake the fish, sprinkle with salt and
pepper. Make a dressing of one-third cup
of butter, three tablespoons of flour and
one pint of milk. When cool add two
beaten eggs. Season with a little finely
minced parsley and a few drops of lemon
juice. In a baking dish put alternate
layers of fish and sauce. Cover with
buttered crumbs and brown.—Mrs James
Wilcox.

Fish in Ramekins

Make a white sauce with two tablespoons of butter, one tablespoon of flour
and one cup of hot milk. Season with
salt and a little curry powder and mix
lightly with about a pound and a half
of halibut, which has been boiled and
flaked. Fill the dishes and cover with

crumbs prepared in the following way:
Melt one-third cup of butter, add one
small cup of dried bread crumbs, mix
well, and salt and pepper to taste. Set
the dishes in the oven to brown the contents and garnish each with a bit of
parsley.

Toasted Codfish

Cut the fish in thin strips and freshen
it. Dry, put between the wires of a
broiler and toast till delicately brown.
Lay on a hot platter and spread well with
butter.

Halibut with Anchovy Sauce

Four tablespoons of butter, four tablespoons of flour, one-eighth teaspoon of
pepper, one-half teaspoon of salt, two
hard-boiled eggs chopped, two cups of
cream, two drops of tabasco, one teaspoon of anchovy essence, one and one-
half cups of cold cooked halibut, flaked.
Mix ingredients in order given and cook
ten minutes. Serve with brown bread
spread with cheese and chopped olives.

Salmon Loaf

Rub a slice of stale bread on a grater
till it is finely crumbled. Put it in a
double boiler with one cup of milk and
steam till you have a smooth paste.
While it is cooking pick over one can of
salmon, taking out every morsel of skin
and bone, then rub the salmon into shreds
with a slitted wooden spoon. To the
panade add half a cup of cream, half a
teaspoon of salt, a dash of cayenne and
the shredded salmon. Mix well and add
three eggs beaten very light. Whip for
a few minutes and pour in a buttered
mold. Set the mold into a pan of hot
water and allow it to bake till firm in a
moderate oven.—Katherine A. French.

Baked Finnan Haddie

Put a haddie in a spider, pour over it
half a cup of milk and half a cup of
water and put at the back of the range,
where it will heat slowly. Let it stand

for half an hour, just barely reaching the simmering point, pour off the liquid, spread with butter and bake twenty-five minutes in a hot oven.

Broiled Finnan Haddie

Put a haddie between the greased wires of a broiler and brown on both sides. Put in a pan, cover with hot water, allow it to stand ten minutes, then drain and put on a platter. Spread with butter and dust with pepper.

Broiled Salt Salmon or Halibut

If very salt freshen for an hour or two in cold water; if merely smoked and slightly salted, wash and cut in small pieces about an inch thick. Season well with pepper and salt, wrap each slice in tough paper well buttered. Twist the ends so the fish is inside a paper bag. Put in a broiler and move over a clear coal fire for about eight minutes. Take the fish from the paper cases and pour over it a good egg sauce.—I. G. C.

Codfish Fritters

Cut the codfish into strips about the size of a finger, freshen by soaking over night in cold water, in the morning dry between towels. Dip each piece in fritter batter and fry delicately brown in hot fat.

Codfish and Potato Omelet

Make a potato and fish mixture exactly as if for fishballs, but leave out the egg. Try out some salt pork in a spider and in the dripping put the fish and potato to cook. When well browned fold in omelet fashion and turn out on a hot platter.

To Bake a Pickerel or Whitefish

Making a stuffing of bread crumbs, butter, pepper, salt, sweet herbs, if preferred, one beaten egg; stuff the fish and sew it, or wind twine around it firmly; lay sticks across the bottom of dripper, to lay the fish on, and bake one and one-half hours slowly.—Mrs Sears, Omaha.

Turbot

Take a fine large whitefish, steam until tender; take out the bones and sprinkle with salt and pepper. For the dressing heat one pint of milk, seasoned with onions, parsley and thyme; then strain and thicken with one-quarter pound of flour. When cool, add two eggs and one-quarter pound of butter. Put in a baking dish a layer of fish, then a layer of sauce, until full; cover the top with bread crumbs, and bake half an hour. —Mrs C. E. Yost, Omaha.

Baked Haddock

Buy a haddock weighing about three pounds. Have the head and tail left on the fish and have it opened underneath for the stuffing, which is made as follows: One cup of cracker crumbs, one saltspoon of salt, one teaspoon of chopped onion, one saltspoon of pepper, one teaspoon of chopped parsley, one teaspoon of chopped pickles, one-fourth cup of butter. This makes a dry, crumbling stuffing. Stuff the fish, sew it up, place two strips of white cotton cloth across the baking pan, stand the fish erect upon the cloth, in the shape of the letter S. Place strips of salt pork on the fish, dredge with flour and baste often with the pork fat. Bake till brown. Remove from the pan by lifting with the strips of cotton. Place upright on a platter. Stick stems of parsley or the ends of celery in the eyes and mouth, garnish with sliced lemon and serve with Hollandaise sauce.

Boiled Fish

Put a piece of oiled paper in the bottom of a fish pan; on it place a large fish that has been cleaned and skinned. Add a sliced onion, two cloves of garlic and sufficient salted water to cover. Boil until done. Take it up and squeeze over it the juice of a lemon. Boil two eggs hard, chop the whites fine and sift the yolks. Cut cold boiled beets in fancy

shapes. Put a row of the chopped whites of eggs down the middle of the fish, on each side of that a row of the yolks and next the yolks a row of the beets. Over all pour a French dressing of oil and vinegar and a drop of mayonnaise on each piece of beet. Garnish the dish with leaves from the heart of a lettuce.

Rechauffe of Fish

Take a pint of cold boiled fish, cut in small pieces. Put into the chafing-dish with two tablespoons of butter, half a cup of milk or cream, a cup of fine cracker or bread crumbs, a little pepper and salt and one egg slightly beaten. Let it simmer for five or six minutes.

Filleting of a Fish

Frequently a fish requires skinning. For this purpose keep a very sharp, thin bladed, fine pointed knife. Cut a narrow strip of skin from along the back, then begin work just below the gills, cutting the skin around, not allowing the knife to penetrate the flesh. When once started— if the fish is fresh—the skin will almost peel off. Keep the blade constantly close to the flesh, so none of it will adhere to the skin. Continue till you have the flesh laid bare to the tail. Turn and skin on the other side. Frequently one wishes to fillet a fish which has been skinned. A small fish weighing two pounds will usually yield four good sized fillets. Slip the keen knife between the flesh and the bones and lift it off cleanly. Cut in two, roll in a small round and skewer with toothpicks. This is a very convenient method of frying, baking or boiling. Fish which comes in steaks, such as cod, swordfish or halibut, may be cut in inch slices and rolled into most sightly fillets.—See Page XXIV.

Frozen Desserts

Peach Bombe

Scald one pint of cream and one and one-half cups of granulated sugar till the mixture looks blue and thin. Take from the fire and add one pint of uncooked cream. When cool add the juice from a pint can of white or pink peaches, one teaspoon of vanilla and one-half teaspoon of peach extract; freeze. When nearly frozen add the peach pulp, mix in thoroughly and pack till you are ready to mold it. Any simple form will do for this, a melon mold is very good. Have it as cold as possible and line it with the ice cream, leaving a cavity in the middle. Fill this with a vanilla mousse, made of one pint of cream, whipped very stiff, four tablespoons of powdered sugar, a few drops of vanilla and the same of orange extract. Put on the cover, bury in ice and salt and leave to ripen for three hours. If you find the outside is not deep enough in color, a suspicion of the damask-rose color paste will improve it.

Maple Dip

Boil down maple syrup, or dissolved maple sugar and water, till it hairs— not quite long enough to wax as for "sugaring off"—but very thick and rich; when just right this is a general favorite.

Caramel

Melt one cup of sugar with one tablespoon of water in a frying pan. Stir till it becomes a dark brown color, but don't burn it. Add one cup of boiling water; simmer ten minutes and cool.

Mixed Fruit

Mix a few peaches cut in bits, juice of two oranges, two slices of pineapple picked fine, two dozen California canned

cherries and one wineglass of sherry; sweeten to taste with sugar, or preferably with sugar syrup—it seems to give more delicacy—and keep the same proportions in making a larger quantity.

Sugar Syrup

Put two cups of sugar and a half cup of water over the fire in a saucepan. Stir until the sugar is dissolved, then let it cook slowly without touching it for about ten minutes, or till it is a clear syrup. Be careful not to use too much before sampling, for it is a great sweetener.—Anne Warner.

Chocolate Pudding (Frozen)

Beat the yolks of three eggs, half a cup of sugar and a level saltspoon of cinnamon together until very light; add slowly a cup of milk heated to boiling, beating well; then pour gradually over an ounce and a half of unsweetened chocolate melted by standing over hot water. Place this mixture in a double boiler and stir constantly until it thickens and coats the spoon. When cold, add a cup of rich cream, vanilla to flavor, and freeze. Prepare and have ready a cup of candied fruits, figs and seeded raisins. Cut the candied fruit and figs in thin slices, the raisins in halves. Make a syrup of a quarter of a cup each of sugar and water, add the fruit, boil until it is tender and plump, then drain. Add the drained fruit to the frozen mixture when it is almost done, and finish freezing. When done, put in a quart melon mold, and let stand an hour or more packed in ice and salt. Whip a cup of cream, sweeten with two tablespoons of sugar, and flavor with either a tablespoon of brandy or of Maraschino.—A. Sulzbacher.

Walnut and Fig Ice Cream

Heat two and a half cups of milk, having reserved cold half a cup to mix with the other ingredients. A part of this half cup of cold milk use for dis-

solving a tablespoon of gelatine and with the rest mix two tablespoons of flour, an egg and a cup of sugar. Into the milk, heating in a double boiler, stir gradually the flour, sugar and egg. When it has come to a custard, add the dissolved gelatine, a cup of rich cream and a teaspoon of vanilla. After you have frozen the mixture add the meats of half a pound of English walnuts, weighed in the shell, and a quarter of a pound of figs. The walnuts and figs should be well chopped. Beat them well in the custard and pack.—Mrs George D. Hale.

Maple Souffle

Three-fourths cup of maple syrup and whites of four eggs. Beat together and cook in a double boiler until thick, stirring constantly. When cool add one pint of cream whipped. Pack in salt and ice for four hours.—Mrs Alvah W. Palmer.

Mint Sherbet

Put ten sprigs of fresh mint to soak for an hour in one cup of half each brandy and sherry. Strain and add three cups of water and two cups of sugar which have been boiled to a syrup, two teaspoons of granulated gelatine dissolved and the whites of four eggs beaten stiff. Freeze stiff.

Fig Ice Cream

Take two tablespoons of gelatine, scald one cup of milk and one cup of vinegar, then add the gelatine, let it dissolve and add one quart of rich cream and freeze. When frozen, add one-fourth pound of chopped figs and one-half pound of chopped English walnuts. Let stand until ready to serve.—Mrs Charles M. Ransom.

Plombiere

One pint of scalded milk, one pint of cream, one teaspoon of gelatine, one handful of stoned raisins, one ounce of citron, shreds of pineapple preserve,

ginger or cherries, four tablespoons of wine, a little extract of almond, whites of four eggs, beaten to a froth, sugar to taste. Freeze as ice cream.—Margaret Sutton Briscoe.

Maple Parfait

Beat four eggs slightly, pour on slowly one cup of hot maple syrup. Cook in double boiler until very thick, stirring constantly. Strain and cool, then add one pint of cream beaten stiff. Mold, pack in salt and ice and let stand three hours.—Fannie M. Farmer.

Peach Sherbet

One quart of peach juice, two cups of sugar, one quart of water, whites of two eggs, juice of one lemon. Boil water and sugar together, add juice of peaches and lemon, and freeze.—Mrs S. R. Van Sant.

Milk Sherbet

Four cups of milk, one and one-half cups of sugar, juice of three lemons, juice of one orange. Mix the juice of the fruit and sugar till half melted, then pour in the milk slowly. If the milk is added too rapidly the mixture may curdle. Freeze in three parts of ice added to one part of salt.—Stella A. Downing.

Maple Ice Cream

One quart of rich cream, one coffee-cup of maple syrup, one-fourth pound of shelled pecans. Chop nuts, add to cream and syrup, and freeze.—Mrs E. Curtis Rumrill.

Cherry Ice Cream

Put one pound of granulated sugar and one-half pint of water in a saucepan over the fire. Stir until the sugar is all dissolved, then let the syrup come to a boil. Drop in gently one quart of white cherries, pitted, and let simmer fifteen minutes. Strain carefully, and when the syrup is cold add one quart of sweet cream and freeze. When it gets rather thick remove the dasher, beat well with

a wooden paddle and stir in the fruit.
Pack and let stand three or four hours
to ripen. Another very nice way to
serve cherry ice cream is to stone and
crush the cherries and add sugar to make
very sweet. Chill on ice. Put a spoonful of the crushed fruit in small glasses
and heap over vanilla ice cream.—Mary
F. Snider.

Cherry Parfait

Add one cup of cherry pulp to two
cups of thick whipped cream and a quarter of a cup of cherries. Flavor with a
few drops of almond extract. Put in a
mold, bury in ice and salt for three hours.
Garnish with candied cherries.

Strawberry Sherbet

Use one quart of berry juice, four
cups of sugar, the juice of two lemons,
three pints of water and a few whole
strawberries. Serve in a punch bowl
with a block of ice, or freeze for frappe.
—Annabel Lee.

Strawberry Parfait

Whip a quart of thick cream with a
small cup of sugar; when stiff mix half
a pint of strawberry juice in carefully.
Turn into an ice cream mold, press the
lid down securely; pack in salt and ice
and freeze for three hours.

Frozen Strawberries

Stem two quarts of ripe strawberries,
put in a bowl with the juice of two
lemons and a pound of sugar; let stand
one hour; mash the berries, pour over a
pint of water, stir until the sugar dissolves, turn into a freezer and freeze.

Iced Strawberry Souffle

Cover two tablespoons of gelatine with
cold water and let soak half an hour;
set over the teakettle and stir until dissolved. Mix a pound of sugar and a
pint of strawberry juice in a saucepan
over the fire until they form a syrup.
Beat the yolks of six eggs until creamy.

Whip a quart of cream. Mix the syrup with the yolks of the eggs in a tin pan and set on ice; strain the gelatine into it and stir carefully until it begins to thicken, then mix the whipped cream in lightly, turn into an ice cream mold, pack in salt and ice and freeze for two hours.

Cherry Mousse

To a pint of double cream add three tablespoons of best confectioner's sugar, a cup of cherry juice and a drop or two of almond extract. Chill on ice, then whip until stiff. Turn into a mold, cover securely and bury in a pan of ice and salt for two hours.—Mary F. Snider.

Strawberry Mousse

Hull a pint of ripe strawberries and rub them through a fine sieve; add a cup of powdered sugar and an ounce of dissolved gelatine; set in a cool place until the mixture begins to thicken. Beat the whites of five eggs and stir them lightly into the mixture. Turn into a wetted mold, cover securely and bury in a tub of finely chopped ice and salt. Set aside for three hours and turn out.

Raspberry Cream in Pineapple Shells

Cut off the top of a large pineapple, then with a strong spoon scoop out the pulp, separating it from the hard core, which should be rejected. Sugar the fruit, let it stand some time, then pour off from it a cup of juice. Trim the pineapple shell at the bottom so it will stand firm and chill in the refrigerator. Mash well a pint of red raspberries, add a fourth of a cup of water, half a cup of sugar and the pineapple juice, and cook the mixture several minutes. Take from the stove, add the juice of a lemon, more sugar if needed, and strain through a cheesecloth. Beat a quart of cream and a cup of sugar until light and frothy, flavor with vanilla and freeze as ice cream; when half frozen add the fruit juice and finish freezing. Fill into the

pineapple shell, set it in a deep mold or the freezer can and let it stand packed in ice and salt for an hour or longer. To serve, lift it from the mold on to a plate covered with a pretty doily, as shown in the illustration.—See Page XXI.

Rose Roll

A dainty cream is the rose roll shown in the illustration. Make one quart of ice cream from any foundation, flavor with one teaspoon of vanilla, one-half tablespoon of rose, color a delicate pink, freeze and line a pound baking powder can, fill center with a chocolate russe mixture made by dissolving one tablespoon of granulated gelatine in one-fourth cup of hot water, add three-fourths cup of powdered sugar and one tablespoon of vanilla; when cool fold in whip from two cups of cream. Cover the top with lining mixture and pack for two hours. Unmold on lace paper, garnish with a pink rosebud and candied rose leaves.—See Page XXII.

Bombe Glace

Make a syrup from two cups of water and one cup of sugar, allowing it to boil for twenty minutes. Then add one cup of the red juice from blood oranges, color it darker if necessary with fruit red. Add two tablespoons of lemon juice and the grated rind of one orange, cool and freeze. Line it into a mold, fill with vanilla ice cream, cover, pack in salt and ice and let it stand two hours.—See Page XXX.

Muskmelon Frappe

Remove the tops of small nutmeg melons so as to form a cover. Take out all the seeds and membrane and scoop out as much of the soft pulp as can easily be removed. Cut this latter into small pieces. Place the seeds and membrane into a sieve to drain the juice, then add the latter to one quart of whipped cream, sweetened; turn this

into an ice cream freezer and turn until stiff. When ready to serve, take the shells, which should have been chilled on ice, place the frappe cream in alternate layers with the melon pulp. Fasten a narrow ribbon looped bow on the lids with long pins; set the melons on lace paper doilies and serve with cake.—See Page XVII.

Angel Stars

Cook one cup of sugar and half a cup of water, pour this slowly into the whites of five eggs beaten stiff, beat until cold, add one quart of cream whipped. Flavor with vanilla and almond, pour into star shaped individual molds, pack and freeze. When serving sprinkle profusely with granulated sugar.—Linda Hull Larned.

Hot Desserts

Queen of Puddings

To a quart of milk, allow a pint of fine bread crumbs, a tablespoon of butter, one cup of sugar and the yolks of four eggs; flavor with the grated rind of a lemon, if liked (or a teaspoon of vanilla extract), and half a teaspoon of salt. Bake in a moderate oven and spread while hot with a layer of any acid jelly or preserves; strained apple juice is sometimes used. Make a meringue of the whites of the eggs and a spoon of powdered sugar, with or without a little lemon juice, and brown in the oven. To be eaten cold without sauce. If a meringue is not liked, three eggs, yolks and whites, may be used in the pudding, and jelly spread upon the top. This variation is good hot.

Tapioca Cocoanut Pudding

Take one-half cup of grated cocoanut with one-half cup of pearl tapioca in cold water to cover. Add one and one-half pints (three cups) of milk, three beaten eggs, one-half cup of sugar and a speck of salt. Mix well and bake in a buttered dish for thirty minutes. Serve hot with cream.

Walnut Pudding

Beat the yolks of three eggs till light and lemon colored. Gradually add to them half a cup of sugar, then one-third of a cup of soft bread crumbs, and a scant half cup of farina. Mix perfectly, fold in the whites of three eggs beaten stiff, and half a cup of broken nut meats. Pour into two layer cake pans which have been buttered and floured. Bake for half an hour in a slow oven. When slightly cooled put the layers together with a creamy sauce made as follows: Cream one-half cup of butter, add grad-

Covington tarts,

Line gem pans with
pastry Fill it 1/3
full of currant jelly.
Put méringue on
top & bake until
pastry is done.

Méringue.

Cream until light
cup brown sugar &
½ cup butter. Add
the beaten yolks of
eggs & beat all
together.

ually one-half cup of sifted powdered sugar and two tablespoons of milk, added drop by drop. Flavor with one tablespoon of brandy. If desired this pudding may be served as it is, or with a sauce for which the following recipe provides:

Mix one-half cup of sugar, one and one-half tablespoons of flour and a dash of salt. Pour over this one cup of boiling water and cook five minutes. Add two tablespoons of butter and vanilla for flavoring. Serve hot. — Katherine A. French.

Cuban Pudding

Crumble a pound of sponge cake with half a pound of grated cocoanut, pour over this a pint of rich cream previously sweetened with loaf sugar and brought to the boiling point. Cover the basin and when the cream is soaked up stir in four well beaten eggs. Butter a pudding mold and arrange four ounces of preserved ginger around it, pour in the pudding carefully and steam for an hour and a half, serve with the syrup from the ginger, which should be warmed and poured over the pudding just before it is served.—Eleanor Marchant.

Prune Shortcake

Sift together, twice, two cups pastry flour, four teaspoons baking powder, one half teaspoon salt and three tablepoons sugar. Blend with this mixture one-half cup butter and add three-quarters of a cup milk mixed with the well-beaten yolks of two eggs. Make into large or individual cakes as desired.

Use best prunes, soak several hours. Then let them cook very slowly, without boiling, until tender but not broken, adding the sugar when half done. To one pint prunes allow two tablespoons sugar and a teaspoon lemon juice. When the prunes are done, remove them carefully and cook the juice until like syrup. On the lower layer of shortcake place prunes

with syrup poured over.   On the top use prunes well drained.   Then heap lightly with whipped cream, slightly sweetened.

Banana Meringue

Place in a baking dish bananas peeled, scraped and cut in quarters, cutting first lengthwise, then across.   Pour over them lemon and pineapple juice, one part lemon to two parts pineapple.   Sprinkle generously with powdered sugar and bake, covered, for one-half hour.   Take from the oven, cover with meringue and brown delicately in a cool oven.

Puffs

Two eggs, one cup of sugar, one-half cup of butter, one cup of sweet milk, two cups of flour, two teaspoons of baking powder, one cup of raisins.   Cream butter and sugar, add beaten eggs, flour and milk, alternately, then raisins rolled in flour.   Steam in small cups half an hour. Serve hot with hard butter sauce flavored with sherry and nutmeg.—Mrs R. P. Bishop, Los Angeles.

Peach Bread Pudding

On a pint of fine stale bread or cracker crumbs pour boiling water and stir in a tablespoon of melted butter.   After standing till thoroughly soaked, add two well beaten eggs and half a cup of sugar. On the bottom of a buttered pudding dish put a thin layer of this batter, over it a layer of sliced peaches, and so on, dredging each layer of peaches with sugar, till the dish is full, having batter at the top.   In a moderate oven about an hour will be required for the baking. Serve with sweetened cream.   This is an excellent way for using second quality peaches.

Peach Manioca Pudding

Into two cups of milk stir four tablespoons of manioca, and let the mixture come to a boil.   Then add two beaten eggs, two tablespoons of sugar, two additional cups of milk, and a bit of lemon peel for flavoring, which will be better

if grated. Pare and slice a dozen peaches, put them into a buttered pudding dish, sprinkle with sugar, and over them pour the manioca mixture, baking till done.—Mrs E. C. Gardner.

Cranberry Pudding

Wash a quart of cranberries, place in a two-quart granite ware saucepan with a pint of water, stew until tender, then add sugar to taste. Take a little more than a half pound of flour, add to this a heaping teaspoon of baking powder and a tablespoon of sugar, mix well together while dry, then add sufficient milk or cream to make a stiff batter, and with this cover the boiling cranberries. Put on the lid of the saucepan and let the pudding cook briskly until the crust is done. Any acid fruits, such as plums, gooseberries, currants or stewed rhubarb, can be used when cranberries are out of season.—Emilia Cowell.

Rice Croquettes

Six ounces of rice and one pint of milk boiled slowly until quite soft, add the grated rind of a lemon, remove from the fire, and mix in while hot one and one-half ounces of butter, one and one-half ounces of sugar, one gill of cold milk and two yolks of eggs stirred in one at a time very hard. Return all to the fire for half a minute, then spread on a dish to cool. When cold, sprinkle a pasteboard with bread crumbs, and form the rice into oblong shapes with a tablespoon, roll in egg, then in the bread crumbs, and then in the egg, and fry in hot fat.

Chocolate Bread Pudding

Soak two cups of bread crumbs in two cups of scalded mlik, add two-thirds cup of sugar, two squares of chocolate previously melted, one teaspoon of vanilla. Mix well and bake in a buttered dish one hour in a moderate oven. Serve hot with whipped cream or hard sauce.

Suet Pudding

One-half cup of milk, one-half cup of chopped suet, one-half cup of molasses, two cups of fruit and nuts chopped together, one cup of flour, pinch of salt, one small teaspoon of soda dissolved in warm water. Steam three hours. Any sort of fruit and nuts may be used.— Eva Snaith Barnes.

English Plum Pudding

Six ounces of fine bread crumbs, two ounces each of lemon, orange and citron peel cut into fine shreds, one-half ounce of mixed spices (cloves, cinnamon, nutmeg), one-fourth pound of chopped apples, one-half teaspoon of minced lemon rind, one-half pound of sugar, three-fourths pound of chopped and seeded raisins, three-fourths pound of currants, one pound of flour, one pound of finely shredded suet. Mix the ingredients thoroughly, then add six eggs and a little milk if needed. This should make a stiff batter. Boil in a pudding basin or mold. Time, five or six hours. —Mrs Jay B. Kline.

Mrs Clarke's Plum Pudding

Use one quart of bread crumbs, one-half cup of molasses, one-half cup of sugar, one cup of raisins, a small piece of citron, one nutmeg, one teaspoon of cinnamon, one-half teaspoon of cloves, three eggs, one cup of sour milk and one-half cup of suet. Steam for three hours.

Baked Apple Dumplings

One cup of butter and lard mixed, one quart of flour, salt to taste, three teaspoons of baking powder. Mix with milk. Pare and core apples. Roll out dough to cover each separately and fill the whole with sugar. Grate nutmeg over the top. Put in the pan with water to half cover. Put in that a half cup of sugar, and butter size of an egg. Baste while baking, allowing three-quarters of an hour, and your dumplings will come

out with a delicious glaced brown crust.
Serve with a hard or a liquid sauce.—
Mrs L. S. Baumgardner.

Christmas Pudding

Take three-quarters of a pound each
of chopped suet, stoned raisins, currants,
sugar and dried bread crumbs, one-
quarter of a pound of sliced citron, two
chopped sour apples and the grated peel
of one lemon. Mix together with one-
half teaspoon each of cloves and salt.
Add six eggs ·and one gill of rum or
brandy. Steam for four hours in two
buttered molds. Turn out on a hot dish,
sprinkle sugar over the pudding, garnish
with a sprig of holly, pour one-half cup
of warm brandy over it and set it on
fire as it goes to the table. Serve with

German Sauce

Mix the yolks of four eggs with one-
eighth of a pound of sugar, add the
grated rind of half a lemon. Stir over
the fire until the mixture coats the spoon.
Serve hot. The pudding may be made
some days before the dinner and
reheated.—Annabel Lee.

Scalloped Apples

Pare a dozen apples and slice thin.
Butter a dish, put in a layer of apples,
then a layer of sugar, cinnamon, butter
and flour, then another layer of apples,
etc, until the dish is full. Bake slowly
for one hour.—Mrs F. B. Kellogg.

Swiss Pudding

Cream half a cup of butter and add
gradually seven-eighths of a cup of flour.
Scald in two cups of milk the grated
rind of one lemon, pour over the first
mixture and cook five minutes in the
double boiler. Beat the yolks of five
eggs till thick and lemon colored, gradually add one-third of a cup of powdered
sugar, add to the cooked mixture and
cool. Fold in the whites of the eggs
beaten to a stiff froth. Turn into a buttered mold, cover, and steam one and a

quarter hours. While steaming be sure that the water surrounds the mold to half its depth.

Plums in Batter

Make a batter with five tablespoons of flour, rather more than a pint of milk, and two eggs. Remove the stones from one pound of large plums, crack them, put the kernels inside of the plums and stir the plums in the batter with two tablespoons of moist sugar. Bake in a hot oven for about three-fourths of an hour. Sprinkle powdered sugar over the top and serve hot.—M. F. Snider.

Cherry Roly Poly

Remove the fiber and skin from five ounces of suet and chop it very fine; add half a pound of flour and one-fourth of a teaspoon of salt; mix well. Add sufficient cold water to make it stick together, and roll out on a well-floured board to the thickness of an inch. Cover well with pitted cherries, dust with sugar and roll quickly; tie in a well-floured cloth, leaving room for it to swell. Place in a kettle of boiling water and keep it boiling steadily for two hours, or it may be steamed for two hours and a half. Serve hot with any nice sweet sauce, or with sweetened cream.

Cherry Souffle

Moisten two tablespoons of flour with a little cold milk, then stir it smoothly into one pint of hot milk. Let it thicken over the fire, then set aside to get cool. Beat the yolks of four eggs light, add two tablespoons of softened butter, a pinch of nutmeg and a sprinkle of cinnamon. Mix in with the thickened milk. Add the whites of the eggs beaten to a stiff froth, one pint of stoned, drained cherries and a gill of thick sweet cream. Flavor with vanilla. Turn into a souffle tin and bake in a quick oven. Serve at once.—M. F. Snider.

Indian Pudding

Scald one quart of milk, when boiling hot stir in three tablespoons of corn meal, the same of flour; wet up with cold milk and one tablespoon of butter. Let cool and add a well-beaten egg, one-half cup of sugar, one-quarter cup of molasses, one-half teaspoon of ginger, one-half teaspoon of cinnamon. Add one-quarter pint of cold milk and bake three hours. Eat with hard sauce.

Individual Strawberry Shortcakes

Mix and sift twice two cups of flour, one-fourth of a cup of sugar, four level teaspoons of baking powder, a pinch of nutmeg and one-fourth of a teaspoon of salt; rub in one-third of a cup of butter; add one egg, well beaten, to two-thirds of a cup of sweet milk. Mix on a floured pastry board, roll, cut with a cookie cutter, and bake in a hot oven twenty minutes. When done split, spread with soft butter, then with well sweetened strawberries. Cover the top layer also with strawberries, sprinkle generously with sugar, and heap over all sweetened whipped cream.—See Page XVII.

Marmalade Pudding

One-half pound of bread crumbs, one-half pound of brown sugar, one-half pound of beef suet cut very fine, four eggs and one small can of marmalade. Mix all together, put in close shape, and boil for three hours.—Mrs W. K. Muir, Detroit.

Cottage Pudding

Cream together one cup of sugar and one-fourth cup of butter; add one beaten egg, two-thirds of a cup of milk, one and one-half cups of flour, sifted with two teaspoons of baking powder. Bake in a buttered tin for thirty to forty minutes. One cup of stoned cherries or berries may be added to this recipe.

Apricot Souffle

Rub enough fruit through a sieve to make three-fourths of a cup of pulp.

Heat in a saucepan and sweeten if needed. Beat the whites of three eggs until stiff and dry, gradually add the hot fruit pulp, and continue beating. Turn into buttered and sugared individual molds, having them three-fourths full; set molds in pan of water and bake until firm in a slow oven.

Peach Darioles

Pare and divide into halves sufficient peaches to make one quart. Add half a cup each of sugar and water, and cook until the peaches are tender. Reserve six of the halves unbroken and rub the remainder through a sieve. Reheat, and when boiling, add a rounded tablespoon of cornstarch, moistened in a little cold water, and cook in a double boiler for ten minutes. Take from the fire, add a tablespoon of lemon juice, a few drops of vanilla, and if not sweet enough, a little more sugar. Beat the whites of two eggs until stiff and dry, and add to them gradually the mixture, while it is still rather hot. Butter six dariole molds, coat with granulated sugar and place half a peach in the bottom of each. Fill about two-thirds full with the mixture and bake about fifteen minutes in a moderate oven. Turn out and serve immediately with sweet cream. If allowed to stand they are apt to fall. Old teacups or deep gem pans make very good substitutes for the dariole molds.

A Quince Pudding

To one pint of flour add two heaping teaspoons of baking powder. Sift together and add two tablespoons of warm butter, a little salt and water enough to make a smooth batter, not too stiff. Stir in one teacup of quince preserves. Bake quickly, sifting sugar over the top when nearly done. Serve with whipped cream well sweetened.—Mrs Kate B. Sherwood.

Jam Pudding

Three eggs, one cup of sugar, one cup of blackberry jam, one-half cup of but-

ter, one dessertspoon of soda dissolved
in hot water, one-half cup of sour milk,
flour enough to make nearly as thick as
cake dough. Bake in a shallow pan and
serve hot with the following sauce:
Two-thirds cup of sugar, butter the size
of an egg, two tablespoons of hot water,
one egg; cream together and set in a
pan of hot water until creamy, being
careful not to let it curdle.—Mrs O. C.
Zinn, Hastings.

Berry Pudding, Steamed

One pint of flour, one teaspoon of baking powder, a pinch of salt. Make into a
soft batter with milk. Put into well-
buttered cups a spoon of batter, then
one of berries, then another of batter.
Steam.

Apple Pudding with Rice

Six sour apples, one cup of cold boiled
rice, one pint of milk, one cup of sugar,
the juice and rind of one lemon, and
yolks of four eggs. Core and chop the
apples; add the boiled rice and milk, beat
the lumps out, add the other ingredients
and bake. Beat the whites of the four
eggs with a little sugar, spread on top
and brown.

Huckleberry Pudding

Butter a pudding dish and line it with
bread, cut in slices half an inch thick
and buttered; remove the crust and cut
the slices to fit the dish. Fill the lined
dish with huckleberries, sprinkle over
them sugar and the grated rind and
juice of a lemon. Place some slices of
buttered bread over the whole. Set the
dish in a pan of water in a hot oven;
cover the pudding with a plate and bake
one and one-half hours. When the pudding is done put roughly over the top
a meringue made of the whites of two
eggs beaten to a stiff froth and two
tablespoons of powdered sugar added to
them. Return to the oven long enough
to brown lightly and serve hot. A sauce
may be served with this pudding or not.

Blueberry Pudding

Beat two eggs light and stir into them one cup of milk and sifted flour enough to make a batter as thick as for pancakes. Put into the flour three teaspoons of baking powder. Butter a mold and put a layer of batter in the bottom, then a layer of blueberries. Alternate the layers until the mold is three-quarters full, cover it closely, and boil one hour. Serve with a rich sauce.

Blackberry Pudding

To make a blackberry pudding, soak two cups of stale bread crumbs in two cups of milk, add a little salt and three well-beaten eggs. Measure one and one-half cups of sifted flour and stir into it half a teaspoon of baking powder, and add to the other ingredients one and one-half pints of blackberries. Put into a buttered pudding dish and steam two hours. Serve with a rich sauce.—Mrs E. C. Gardner.

Invalid Cookery

Prune Jelly

Stew a cup of prunes in sufficient water to cover them well. When tender pour through a potato press or a colander, add an ounce of gelatine previously soaked for half an hour in a little water, return to the fire, sweeten to taste, let cook three minutes and pour in molds to cool.

Apple and Custard

Pare and core a large apple, fill the cavity with sugar. Put a little water in the bottom of a dish and bake. Make a custard of a cup of milk, a heaping teaspoon of sugar, a small teaspoon of cornstarch, yolk of one egg. Flavor to taste after boiling thick and pour around the baked apple. Use the white for a meringue; eat cold.

Slip

One tablespoon of cornstarch, a pint of boiling water, one small cup of sugar, juice and rind of one lemon. Boil till thick and pour in a baking dish. Beat the white of an egg with a tablespoon of sugar spread on top, brown slightly and serve cold with cold boiled custard.

Fruit Blancmange

A cup of any fruit juice, fresh or canned, heated, sweetened to taste and thickened with a tablespoon of cornstarch. Cook well and serve cold with milk. If a little less cornstarch is used, and, when nearly cold, the stiffly beaten white of an egg is added, a delicious float is the result. All juices should be strained.—Mary M. Willard.

Egg Cream

Two eggs, two tablespoons of sugar, juice and grated rind of half a lemon. Separate yolks from whites of eggs and

beat with sugar in bowl until both are
well mixed, then add lemon juice and
rind and place the bowl in a dish of
boiling water on the stove   Stir slowly
until the mixture begins to thicken, then
add beaten whites of eggs and stir for
two minutes, or until the whole resembles
very thick cream. Remove from the fire
and pour into a small pudding dish and
cool.   Serve in small dainty cups or
glasses.—Mrs John A. Oberg, Rockford.

Gruel for Invalids

Put a pint of water on the stove and
as it heats stir in two tablespoons of
oatmeal and a pinch of salt. When the
gruel is well boiled, break an egg into
a bowl and beat it light with enough
sugar to sweeten it; pour the boiling
gruel on the egg and sugar, and beat
hard.   A wineglass of sherry may be
added if desired.—Mrs Sarah N. Mc-
Candless, Pittsburg.

Rice Water

Two tablespoons of rice, one quart
of boiling water.   Simmer two hours,
strain, add a pinch of salt, sugar and
brandy to taste. Use either hot or cold.
A few raisins can be boiled in with the
rice sometimes.

Beef Tea and Oatmeal

A tablespoon of well-cooked oat-
meal and a cup of beef broth to thin it.
Season to taste; serve hot with toast.—
M. M. Willard.

Sponge Cake

Two cups of sifted flour, one and a
half cups of pulverized sugar, a half cup
of cold water, two tablespoons of lemon
juice, two teaspoons of baking powder,
four eggs. Beat the yolks, add sugar,
half to yolks and half to whites; when
both have been well beaten, stir gently
together and then add water and flour.
Do not beat, and bake till the cake leaves
the side of the pan. This is the "inva-

lid's own," and is very good, no matter how dry it becomes.

Blancmange

One and a half tablespoons of cornstarch, one of sugar, a pint of milk, a pinch of salt. Let the milk come to a boil; add the starch, dissolved in a little cold water, salt and sugar. Stir till thick, then cook for thirty minutes in a double boiler. When it has partly cooled, add a beaten egg and any flavoring desired. Serve with milk when cold.

Tapioca Jelly

One-half cup of tapioca, two cups of water, one-half cup of sugar, juice and rind of one-half lemon. Cook the tapioca in the water for one hour, using a double boiler. At the end of that time add the lemon and sugar, and three teaspoons of brandy. Strain and serve cold with milk. This is one of the few things for the sick of which enough can be prepared for several meals.

Cracker Pudding

A cup of milk, one tablespoon of cracker crumbs, yolk of one egg. Bake and make a meringue of the white and a generous tablespoon of sugar. Flavor with vanilla and serve with sweetened milk.

Baked Custard

One egg beaten light, a scant pint of milk, two teaspoons of sugar. Pour in a small buttered pan, grate nutmeg over the top, set in a larger pan of boiling water, and bake in a moderate oven. Watch it or it will cook too much. Insert a knife blade and if it comes out clean the custard is done. Serve ice cold.

Chocolate Pudding

A cup of milk, a scant cup of bread crumbs, one tablespoon of dry cocoa and same of sugar mixed together, yolk of one egg. Bake in moderate oven. Make

a meringue of the white and a tablespoon
of pulverized sugar. Serve either hot
or cold with milk.

Orange Pudding

One-half cup of sugar, two tablespoons of rolled cracker crumbs, one egg,
one small orange (grate the rind of half
only), a pint of milk or water. Bake
like custard and serve cold.—Mary M.
Willard.

Ham Toast

Mix with one tablespoon of finely
chopped ham the beaten yolk of an egg
and a little milk. Heat over the fire
without boiling. Spread on thin buttered toast.

Omelet

Beat one egg separately, the white
till stiff, but not dry. Add one tablespoon of milk to the yolk, mix well,
stir in the white and pour at once into
a hot buttered pan. Set in a quick
oven till a delicate brown. Loosen the
edges, lift up one end with a cake turner,
fold over and serve at once. This
omelet does not toughen or get heavy.

Shirred Egg

Beat one egg very slightly with a
fork, add a tablespoon of milk, and
mix. Pour into a hot pan where a
teaspoon of butter has melted. Stir
constantly with the fork until thick and
creamy. Serve on hot buttered toast.

Sweet Rolls

One quart of potatoes, boiled and
mashed. Add one cup of sweet milk,
two eggs beaten light, one scant cup of
sugar, a teaspoon of salt, and flour
enough to make a thin batter. Let rise.
When light, make into a stiff dough and
let rise again, then make into light rolls.
Bathe the tops with milk, sprinkle with
cinnamon and bake quickly. No shortening is needed, and they must be kept
twenty-four hours before using. Then

slice, butter thinly, and toast before a bed
of glowing coals. These will be good
as long as they last.—Mary M. Willard.

Milk Soup

A pint of boiling milk poured over
three tablespoons of fine cracker or
bread crumbs. Salt to taste.

Syllabub

Dissolve a generous teaspoon of sugar
in a tablespoon of brandy. Put in a
pint cup and milk into this from the cow
till the foam reaches the top.

Beef Broth and Egg

Make a good broth and pour over a
well-beaten egg. Season with salt and
serve with a slice of delicately browned
toast.

Egg Water

Stir the whites of two eggs in a half
glass of ice water. Add salt or sugar
to taste. This is especially good for
bowel troubles.

Apple Water

Six sour, juicy apples; slice in a stone
pitcher, add a tablespoon of sugar and
pour over it one quart of boiling water.
Cover closely, and when cold, strain.
Mildly laxative.

Bran Tea

This is so good and nutritious it ought
to be more widely used. Add one pint
of boiling water to one-half pint of wheat
bran. Let stand on the back of the stove
for an hour, but do not boil. Strain and
serve with sugar and cream same as
coffee.

Potato Soup

One generous tablespoon of mashed
potato. Add gradually a pint of new
milk. Place on the stove and when hot
stir in a heaping teaspoon of cornstarch dissolved in cold milk. Let boil
up several times. Season with salt and
celery salt, or a sprig of parsley. The

potatoes must be free from lump. Rice
may be substituted if liked, but must also
be mashed and the milk added slowly.—
M. M. Willard.

Posset

Boil a cup of milk and stir in one
tablespoon of molasses. Let boil up
well, strain and serve.

Milk and Albumen

A pint of new milk, unbeaten whites
of two eggs, a small pinch of salt. Put
in a clean quart bottle, cork and shake
hard for five minutes.

Meats and Poultry

Veal Souffle

Make a sauce of one tablespoon of butter, one tablespoon of flour, one cup of hot milk or stock, half a teaspoon of salt and a few grains of pepper. Add one cup of chopped veal and one-fourth cup of stale bread crumbs. Remove from the fire, add the yolks of two eggs beaten light. Fold in the whites beaten stiff. Bake thirty minutes in a buttered mold set in a pan of hot water in a moderate oven.

Frankforts in Cream Sauce

Make a cream sauce of one and a half tablespoons each of butter and flour and one cup of milk. Season with pepper and salt. Skin four Frankfort sausages. Cut into pieces about an inch long and bring them to the boiling point in the sauce.—Stella A. Downing.

Chicken Pudding

One-half pound of flour, one quart of milk, four eggs, six ounces of butter, one large or two small chickens. Season very highly with pepper and salt. Serve immediately upon baking. Line the dish with the chicken, pour batter over it. Have the dish hot before the chicken is put in.—Margaret Sutton Briscoe.

Spiced Beef (or Beef a la Mode)

One piece of the round of beef (known as the "pot roast"), weighing from three to five pounds. Put two tablespoons of butter in a stewing kettle over a hot fire; when butter melts, brown the meat on both sides. Remove the meat temporarily and add flour to the butter; let it brown and thicken, then add three pints of boiling water, one bay leaf, one sprig of celery, some parsley, and one large onion with a clove stuck in it,

two carrots, one turnip, one tablespoon of salt and one shake of pepper. Replace the meat in this liquid at once and let it simmer for at least six hours. Turn the meat over and stir it occasionally. The secret of the success with this dish is slow cooking. When finished it should be as tender as bread. Place the meat on a hot platter, strain the gravy over it and serve garnished with sliced boiled carrots and sprigs of parsley. The gravy should be thick and of a dark brown color.—Mrs William Hutton Blauvelt.

Duck

Pick, singe and wipe outside. Salt and pepper the inside after carefully drawing and wiping out with a piece of old linen. Do not wash them. Cut off the wings at the second joint and truss the duck neatly. Roast in a *very* hot oven from fifteen to twenty minutes, in a baking pan containing a little water; baste frequently. Celery or onions, or apples, cored and quartered, are sometimes placed inside the duck to improve the flavor.

Meat Loaf

Two pounds of chopped beef, one pound of chopped pork, two eggs, four teaspoons of milk, five crackers, roll fine, salt and pepper. Mix in loaf with bits of butter on top. Bake one hour.—Mrs Henry N. Wilson.

Creamed Chicken

One chicken of four and one-half pounds or two of six pounds, four sweetbreads, and one can of mushrooms. Boil chicken and sweetbreads, and when cold cut up as for salad. In a saucepan put four coffeecups or one quart of cream; in another four large tablespoons of butter and five even ones of flour. Stir the latter until melted, then pour on the hot cream, stirring until it thickens; add and stir in a small half of a grated onion and a very little nutmeg, and season highly with black and red pepper.

Put chicken and ingredients together, with sweetbreads and mushrooms (which if large should be cut in four pieces), in a baking dish, cover with bread crumbs and piece of butter, and bake twenty minutes. It can be made without sweetbreads by using more chicken, but it is not so good.—Mrs Edgar E. Bartlett, Rockford.

Chicken Terrapin

Make a sauce with two level tablespoons of butter, two of flour and one cup of cream, or half cream and chicken stock. Season with salt and pepper. When boiling hot remove from the fire, add two well-beaten eggs and one pint of chopped cold chicken. Butter individual dishes or one baking dish, pour in the chicken mixture and place the dishes in a pan of hot water. Spread crumbs on the top and bake in a moderate oven for twenty minutes. Serve at once.

Baked Ham

Soak the ham in cold water over night (old hams require two nights and a day). After soaking, scrape well. Make a quart of flour into a very stiff paste and cover the entire skin side; place the ham perfectly level in a roasting pan and fill pan with cold water. Replenish occasionally with hot water while baking. For a seven to eight-pound ham bake about three and one-half hours; for one weighing eight to ten pounds four to five hours.

Chicken Pie Crust

Sift together two and one-quarter quarts of flour, two and one-half teaspoons of baking powder, one-half teaspoon of salt. Rub into the flour one cup of lard and one-third pound of butter. Moisten with one pint of milk. Place on a board and roll in one and two-thirds pounds of butter in four rollings. Line the sides of the dish and arrange four chickens stewed until nearly tender,

with the largest bones removed. Cover
with the remaining crust, cut an opening
in center for the steam to escape.

Imperial Scallop

One cup of chopped ham, one and one-
half cups of cream sauce, three hard-
boiled eggs, one-half cup of fresh bread
crumbs, with a large teaspoon of melted
butter. Stir the chopped ham in cream
sauce, put one-half in a baking dish, add
the chopped eggs, then the rest of ham,
cover with bread crumbs, and bake until
it is a very light brown.—Miss A.
Waring.

Frizzled Beef

Use a quarter of a pound of dried
beef, tender, crimson and shaved very
fine. Into the pan put one tablespoon of
butter, let it melt, then add one and one-
half tablespoons of flour. Rub to a
smooth paste, pour in one cup of thin
cream, add a dash of paprika, then the
beef. Allow it to boil up, then serve on
rounds of toast.

Roast Turkey

Remove the crusts from a stale loaf of
bread. Break the loaf in the middle and
grate or rub the bread into fine crumbs.
Season highly with salt and pepper. Add
a cup of diced celery, cooked tender.
With a fork mix celery and seasoning
well through the crumbs, then sprinkle
over and through them three or four
tablespoons of melted butter. With a
spoon put the prepared crumbs in the
place from which the crop was removed
until the breast becomes plump. Put
the remaining crumbs in the body. Do
not pack the crumbs closely in either crop
or body, but allow room for them to
swell when moistened by the steam from
the turkey in cooking. Fold back the
wings. Press the legs close to the body,
crossing the drumsticks in front of the
tail. With small skewers and strong
cord fasten in proper shape. Place the
turkey, back up, on a rack in the roasting

pan. When the back is browned turn the turkey over, and when the breast and sides are nicely browned, baste with a thin gravy every ten or fifteen minutes until the fowl is cooked. An eight-pound turkey will cook thoroughly in two hours. Use the water in which the celery was cooked to make basting gravy for the turkey.—Emma P. Ewing.

Lamb Terrapin

Take slices of the meat which have been left and cut into fine dice. Two cups of these dice will be required to feed a party of eight. Make a sauce in the chafing-dish, using two tablespoons of butter, one tablespoon of flour, one teaspoon of mustard, one tablespoon of currant jelly, one tablespoon of Worcestershire sauce, a dash of paprika and salt, one cup of white stock, a quarter cup of cream and the yolks of three hard-boiled eggs pressed through a potato ricer. Beat this with a whisk till smooth, add the diced lamb, allow it to boil up, then sprinkle in the whites of the eggs cut fine and two tablespoons of sherry. Serve on slices of buttered brown bread toast.

Roast Lamb

Wipe the meat with a damp towel, place in a baking pan, and dredge with pepper. Add a cup of boiling water and a teaspoon of salt to the pan. Baste every ten minutes, and let bake fifteen minutes to the pound in a very hot oven. When done take up on a heated dish, garnish with cress and serve with mint sauce and green peas.

Boiled Quarter of Lamb

Take a plump hind leg, put into a kettle and cover with boiling water. Set over the fire and let come to a boil, pour in a pint of cold water and let simmer gently until done. Take the meat up on a hot dish, garnish with boiled cauliflower and serve with caper sauce.

Braised Shoulder of Lamb

Bone a shoulder of lamb, leave the knuckle and fill the cavity with a rich bread stuffing; tie it neatly in shape and wrap in a buttered paper. Lay in a deep pan with two ounces of butter, a sliced carrot and turnip each, an onion stuck with cloves and a bunch of sweet herbs. Pour over sufficient stock to cover the bottom of the pan. Set over a slow fire and let simmer gently, baste every ten minutes. When nearly done lift from the pan, remove the paper; brush the meat with melted glaze and set in the oven to brown. Take up the shoulder on a heated dish. Strain the gravy and pour around it. Garnish with a puree of green peas and serve with maitre d'hotel sauce.

Veal Loaf

Chop very fine four pounds of raw lean veal, a quarter of a pound each of ham and salt pork. Mix with the meat one cup of stale bread crumbs soaked in milk, a quarter of a cup of melted butter, one teaspoon each of salt, paprika and onion juice, one-quarter teaspoon each of all-spice, cloves and nutmeg, the grated rind and juice of one lemon and two well-beaten eggs. Press into a buttered bread pan and cover the top with lardoons of salt pork; bake one hour. Cut when cold into thin slices.

Beef Loaf

Put three pounds of round steak with a few bones into two quarts of cold water, season with one teaspoon of salt and cook till tender. Allow the meat to cool in the liquor. Remove the meat, rejecting the bones and skin, and put through a meat chopper, using the medium knife. Boil the liquor till it is reduced to two cups, then put in the meat, one-fourth teaspoon of paprika, juice and grated rind of one lemon, two table-spoons of vinegar, quarter of a teaspoon each of ground cloves, allspice and nut-

meg. Pour the mixture into a buttered mold and set in the refrigerator to cool. Turn out on a platter, cutting in neat slices. Serve with it beet salad.

Fried Chicken

Clean and wash a chicken of the frying size, twice the age of a broiler; cut it up, dividing the breast into two pieces, and lay it in cold water for half an hour. Have on the stove a frying pan with lard an inch deep in it. Season the chicken well with salt and pepper, and dredge well with flour. Drop into the boiling lard and turn frequently till it is beautifully brown. It must not cook done on one side before turning on the other, as it will not be so evenly and nicely cooked. Maryland cooks often invert a pan over the frying chicken in order to cook it in the very best way.—Marian V. Dorsey.

Stuffed Ham

Take a well-smoked ham and boil it till it is about half done. Let it get cold and skin it. Then get a good parcel of cabbage sprouts, a handful of parsley, a small piece of stale bread, and chop them all up together, with plenty of black pepper. Make gashes in the ham with a sharp knife about an inch apart from the hock down clear across the ham and then stuff it to the bone. Bake till done, say an hour or two.—Margaret Sutton Briscoe.

Veal Cutlets

Cut slices of veal in pieces for serving, sprinkle with salt and pepper, dip in flour, egg and crumbs and fry slowly, until well browned, in salt pork fat or butter. Pour over one and a half cups of brown sauce, and cook slowly on the back of the range until tender. Arrange on hot platter and strain sauce around cutlets; garnish with parsley.

Brown Sauce: Brown three tablespoons of butter, add three tablespoons of flour and stir until well browned. Add

gradually one and a half cups of brown stock or water. Season with salt, pepper, lemon juice and kitchen bouquet. The trimmings and bones from the cutlets may be put on with one and a half cups of cold water, allowed to boil slowly, strained and used for stock in the sauce. —Miss Stella A. Downing.

Pan-broiled Steak

Remove extra fat from the meat. Heat a frying pan very hot without any fat. Sear the meat on both sides, then cook more slowly until done. Steak one inch thick should be cooked five minutes. Season and serve on a hot platter.

Snowball Croquettes

Prepare chicken croquettes in the usual way, but with the white meat only, remembering that this will absorb more sauce in mixing than when the whole fowl is used. Form into round balls, dip in crumbs, egg and crumbs again. Stick all over them, every quarter-inch or so, pieces of gelatine as it comes from the box. You can vary these croquettes farther by rolling in the center of each one an oyster, parboiled and dried, a slice of truffle or a piece of sweetbread which has been cooked and seasoned.

Make a white sauce of three-quarters of a cup of cream and the same of water in which the fowl was cooked. Season to taste with salt, cayenne, celery salt and onion juice, and thicken in the usual way. Add, in this case, just a touch of damask-rose color paste.—Anne Warner.—See Page XXIII.

Rice and Chicken Croquettes

One cup of cold chicken, chopped fine and seasoned with salt and pepper, one cup of cold boiled rice. Heat both together in a double boiler, adding a little milk, if the mixture seems dry. When hot, stir in one egg beaten light, and when it is thoroughly mixed, remove from the fire. When the mixture is cold, form into croquettes, roll in egg, then in

fine bread or cracker crumbs and again
in egg, and fry in hot lard.

Italian Stew

Fry out a slice of salt pork. Have
three pounds of beef for a pot roast cut
in pieces; brown these in the pork fat.
Put the meat in a large saucepan without
water, add four onions cut in pieces, six
tomatoes peeled and sliced (canned tomatoes will do), and a bunch of sweet herbs
and parsley chopped fine, with a spoon of
salt. Cover and stew four or five hours
on the back of the stove. The cover
should be tight, and the process slow,
until the vegetables have melted away,
and the meat is tender.

Roasted Turkey

Stuff two small hen turkeys with
either mushrooms, chestnuts or oysters.
If mushrooms or chestnuts are used, boil
them until tender, mince them with their
liquor, mix with bread crumbs, butter,
salt, pepper and cream. If oysters are
used, parboil them slightly, mince them
and use their liquor. Skewer legs of
the turkeys close to the bodies, tuck their
necks into the breast openings, spread the
turkeys with a paste of butter and flour,
add salt and pepper and cover with
stalks of celery, using both the white and
greenish-white parts. Add a little hot
water to pan and baste frequently. Lay
tiny sausages around the turkeys the last
hour, remove celery to brown the turkeys.
Bake them two hours, then serve them
on a platter neck to neck and garnish
them with the sausages, watercress and
lady apples, putting one cored apple on
the end of each short drumstick.

Cook one tablespoon of butter with a
teaspoon each of minced onion, carrot,
parsley and celery, add a bit of thyme,
tiny piece of bay leaf, a few peppercorns
and three tablespoons of flour, when
boiling add the strained liquor from the
pan and the giblets boiled and minced.
Strain and serve in a boat.—Linda Hull
Larned.

Jellied Chicken with Mayonnaise

One five or six-pound chicken, one can of French mushrooms, one small onion, six cloves, four hard-boiled eggs, twelve olives, three tablespoons of capers, one package of gelatine. Put the chicken, cloves and onion in three pints of cold water; season with salt and pepper, and boil slowly. When tender, take off and let the chicken and broth get cold. Then cut the chicken in dice-shaped pieces and season; skim the cold broth, removing all the fat. Put the gelatine in a little more than a cup of the broth; place the rest of the broth on the fire with about three-fourths of a cup of the mushroom juice, let come to a good scald, then pour the hot broth on the dissolved gelatine. Curl the olives and cut the eggs and a few of the mushrooms in thin slices and decorate the bottom of the mold, then lay the minced chicken in carefully (lightly), adding a few of the mushrooms from time to time. Strain the broth and pour on just enough to cover well. Set away to harden. Serve with mayonnaise dressing.—Mrs F. B. Kellogg.

Roast Goose

Select a young goose weighing eight to ten pounds. Wash and scrub the skin thoroughly and cleanse with warm water. Wipe the fowl dry and stuff with six potatoes boiled and mashed, mixed with one teaspoon of salt, one-half teaspoon of white pepper, one teaspoon of sage, one tablespoon of onion juice and two tablespoons of butter. Never stuff poultry of any kind full, but leave some room for the stuffing to swell. Sew and truss the goose and steam it for one-half hour to draw out the oil. Then place in a pan, dredge with salt, pepper and flour and roast in the oven, pouring in a little hot water when it begins to brown, and basting often. Cook for about one hour and a half, or until brown and tender. Remove the goose to a hot platter, pour off the oil in the pan and make a brown

gravy with flour and water, as for roast turkey. Garnish the goose with celery tops or cress, and serve with brown gravy in a gravy boat, and cider apple sauce.

Sweet Potato Stew

Cut a pound of round steak into small pieces, put into a granite ware saucepan, cover with hot water and place on the stove. When about to boil, remove the cover and carefully skim off the dark scum which will rise to the top. Put a small piece of butter and salt and pepper to taste, two or three onions cut small and the same number of tomatoes. Then pare and cut up three or four sweet potatoes and with these completely cover the other ingredients. Allow it to boil quickly for a few minutes, then simmer for two or three hours. This stew will bear reheating, as the sweet potatoes never become sodden like their Irish cousins.—Emelia Cowell.

Hash

Three-eighths cup of cooked meat cut into cubes, one-fourth cup of cold boiled potatoes cut into cubes; cook one-fourth teaspoon of fat and one-half teaspoon of flour in a stewpan until brown, add one-half cup of cold stock or water and season with a teaspoon of onion juice and pepper and salt. When this gravy is the proper consistency then turn in the cubes of meat and the potatoes, and when thoroughly heated serve with toasted crackers or bread, with parsley as garnish.

Breast of Lamb Broiled

Trim a breast of lamb and put it in a saucepan, cover with stock, add a bunch of sweet herbs, a slice of onion, a piece of mace and two or three cloves; set over the fire to simmer gently until tender. Take up, dredge with salt and pepper, brush over with beaten egg and grated cracker and broil over a clear fire until brown on both sides. Take up on a

heated dish, pour over a little melted butter, garnish with asparagus tips and serve with brown caper sauce.

Breaded Chops

Cut a loin of lamb into chops three-quarters of an inch thick. Dip each one in beaten egg and lay on a meat board. Mix a teacup of grated bread crumbs with a saltspoon of salt, a pinch of black pepper, a tablespoon of minced parsley and a little grated nutmeg. Roll the chops in the bread crumbs and fry in boiling fat until a light brown. Take up on a heated dish and garnish with slices of lemon and sprigs of parsley.

Lamb's Head

Clean the head and put in a pot with the liver. Cover with water, add a teaspoon of salt, and let boil until tender. Take up the head, split it through the bone, cut the meat across both ways, put in a dripping pan, spread with grated bread crumbs seasoned with salt, pepper, nutmeg and sweet herbs. Set in the oven, baste every few minutes with melted butter. Chop the liver and tongue, put in a saucepan with half a teacup of the water in which the head was boiled, set over the fire, thicken with a teaspoon of butter rolled in flour, season with salt and pepper; let come to a boil. Take the head up on a heated dish, pour the liver and tongue around it, garnish with slices of lemon, and serve.

Hot Pot (An English dish)

Take two pounds of the neck of a lamb, cut up the meat, take out all the bones. Butter a deep baking dish. Line the bottom and sides with thin slices of potato. Quarter the lamb kidneys and put in the dish, then add the meat, season with salt, pepper, a little finely chopped mint and a few drops of onion juice. Cover the top with sliced potatoes, pour over half a pint of stock, cover the dish and set in a moderate oven to

bake for an hour and a half. **Serve**
very hot.

Lamb Kidney en Brochette

Take four lambs' kidneys, cut nearly
through, take out the white veins and
trim off the fat. Wash well in cold
water, put in a small saucepan and cover
with boiling water, let stand near the fire
for five minutes, take out and wipe dry.
Slice fat bacon very thin in pieces the
size of the half of each kidney. Place a
piece of kidney on a skewer, then a slice
of bacon, then the kidney and bacon
until the kidney is all used. Arrange on
a broiler, baste with melted butter. Broil
over a clear fire for six or eight minutes.
Dust with salt and pepper and serve very
hot on the skewers.

Chicken, Baltimore Style

Split a young chicken down the back
as for broiling; take out the breastbone
and cut off the tips of the wings. Cut
into four pieces, dredge with salt and
pepper, dip them in egg and crumbs and
put in a pan with enough melted butter
poured over each piece to moisten it.
Roast in a hot oven about twenty minutes. Make a rich cream sauce or
Bechamel sauce, pour on a dish and place
the chicken on it. Garnish with slices
of fried bacon.—Anne Warner.

Roasted Pork Tenderloin

Take two tenderloins and split lengthwise. Place two together and fill with
dressing made of bread, onion, egg, sage
and seasoning. Wind a string around to
keep them together. Season on the outside and tack on with toothpicks three
slices of bacon. Roast as you would any
other roast, about forty-five minutes.
This will make a nice cold meat dish
sliced.—Mrs W. A. Chapman.

Sauerkraut with Spareribs (German way)

Cover the kraut with cold water, add a
little salt if necessary, and place on to

boil fully three hours before using it. About one hour before it is done, put your spareribs in and let them boil until they fall freely from the bones. Remove the spareribs, and stir in the kraut a grated raw potato from which you have allowed the water to run. Let it come to a boil after this, being careful that it doesn't burn on; remove from stove and serve.—Mrs W. A. Chapman.

Chicken en Coquille

Boil chicken in water or broth. Cut the meat into small dice and mix hot with a hot Bechamel sauce. Place in shells, sprinkle over cracker crumbs with bits of butter, and brown in hot oven. Mushrooms added to the chicken improve them.—Mrs R. P. Bishop, Los Angeles.

Fillet of Pork

Take pork tenderloin, split lengthwise on the side, place two cut parts together, filling with bread stuffing; bind with coarse thread to keep together; place in baking pan on bed of vegetables and spices, including one-half carrot, one-half onion, allspice and cloves; cover the meat with fat pork or bacon, place in hot oven top grate for ten minutes; return to lower oven, cook three-quarters of an hour, or until done, baste frequently with a little butter and water, garnish with stewed apples and cress.

Veal Pie

Stew knuckle of veal an hour and a half; pick off the meat. Make sauce of equal quantities of butter and flour, stir into the boiling veal stock and season with pepper and salt, a few drops of onion juice and a little celery salt. For the pie crust, take two cups of pastry flour, one-half teaspoon of salt, two teaspoons of baking powder, two tablespoons of shortening, one egg, and nearly a cup of milk. Sift baking powder and flour, add salt, the beaten egg and milk, pouring round outside. Mix with two forks, as it makes it lighter.

Pour the mixture on boiling hot meat and gravy. Bake in hot oven.—Agnes Pitman.

Veal Ragout

Take a breast of veal. Lay it in a baking kettle and cover with water. Slice one onion, a little powdered sweet marjoram, salt and pepper, also a little clove. Let this boil slowly until tender, then pour off your liquor; then dredge it with flour and butter, place in the oven and baste with butter and water, sprinkling cracker crumbs over it.—Mrs William Edwards.

English Beefsteak Pie

Take a round steak, not too thick, cut it in narrow strips, then in short pieces, two inches in length. Do not use fat. Put these pieces of beef in the bottom of a four-pound butter crock, only enough to cover bottom of crock. Over this put a good sprinkling of sifted flour, salt and pepper and lastly lumps of good butter. Then put another layer of the pieces of beef, with the addition of the flour, salt, pepper and butter, and so continue until the meat is all in the crock with a generous sprinkling of flour, lumps of butter and salt and pepper on top. More than cover this with cold water, then a plate on top of crock, and place in the oven for four and a half or five hours, replenishing with hot water as it cooks down dry, as this will make a delicious and rich gravy to be served with the meat when cooked, poured over a hot shortcake or rich biscuit crust, split and cut in squares, placed on a deep hot platter. Pour the meat and gravy over this and serve hot. Some of the gravy can be reserved for the gravy boat if desired. There will be plenty of gravy if the meat is kept well covered with hot water while cooking.—Mrs Wilson B. Chisholm.

Sweetbreads, Plain

Let sweetbreads stand in cold water for thirty minutes. Remove membranes.

Cook in boiling salted water for twenty
minutes and then put them in cold water
to harden. Cut in small pieces, place
either in chafing-dish or griddle, with
large lump of butter, and cook until
brown.—Mrs Dickson Moore.

Curried Chicken

Four tablespoons of butter, two cups
of rich milk, four tablespoons of flour,
two cups of chicken meat, one tablespoon
of curry powder, two hard-boiled eggs,
one teaspoon of onion juice, salt and pepper. Melt butter, add flour and curry
powder mixed, onion juice and milk,
cook five minutes, add chicken and eggs
and seasonings, cook until chicken is hot.
Turkey or lamb may be prepared in the
same way.

Sweetbreads en Casserole

Clean two pairs of sweetbreads. Cook
in boiling, salted, acidulated water fifteen
minutes, then plunge into cold water,
after which break or cut into pieces.
Melt three tablespoons of butter in an
omelet pan, add one-quarter cup of onion,
one-quarter cup of carrot cut fine, cook
three minutes, then add the sweetbreads.
When nicely browned put into the casserole, add a bit of bay leaf, two cups of
white stock, salt and pepper to taste,
cover and cook slowly for half an hour.
Shape a dozen potato balls with a French
vegetable cutter, fry in two tablespoons
of butter, add the caps of a dozen fresh
peeled mushrooms and combine with the
contents of the casserole, adding more
stock if necessary. Cook fifteen minutes,
then remove the cover to brown the
sweetbreads. Re-cover and serve in the
casserole.

Mutton Chops en Casserole

Melt two tablespoons of butter, add
three slices of onion, and saute in it the
chops cut from a shoulder of mutton.
Place in a casserole one-quarter cup each
of carrots, turnips, celery and onion, lay
the chops on top of the vegetables and

add one cup of stock or hot water. Cover and cook about one and one-half hours, season with salt and pepper, add three potatoes cut in slices and parboiled and more stock if necessary. Cover and cook until tender. Remove cover to brown the chops and potatoes. Serve from the casserole.

Rabbit en Casserole

Dress the rabbit and cut into pieces for serving, dredge with flour and fry in butter until delicately browned, then put into the casserole. Melt two tablespoons of butter in the frying pan, add an onion cut in slices, and when well browned add two tablespoons of flour and slowly add two cups of hot water, stir until smooth, then pour over the rabbit, add a bit of bay leaf, enough water to half cover and salt and pepper to taste. Cover and let cook in the oven slowly for an hour or more. When tender add one and one-half tablespoons of lemon juice, three tablespoons of sherry. Cover and serve at once. If a thicker sauce is desired add another tablespoon of flour.

Chicken en Casserole

Dress a young chicken and cut in pieces for serving. Melt three tablespoons of butter in an omelet pan, add an onion and a small carrot, each cut in slices, add the chicken and cook until delicately browned. Remove to the casserole, add one and one-half cups of white stock and a bit of bay leaf. Cover and let cook an hour or until nearly tender, then add some potatoes cut in slices and a few mushrooms sauted in butter, season with salt and pepper and cook until tender. Add three tablespoons of sherry and serve at once.

Squabs en Casserole

Draw, clean and truss six squabs, saute in three tablespoons of butter, then remove to the casserole, half cover with hot water or stock, add a bit of bay leaf, a

sprig of parsley and cook until almost tender, then add two dozen potato balls, sauted in butter with one sliced onion. When the potatoes are tender add the yolks of three eggs beaten and diluted with three-quarters cup of thin cream. As soon as the sauce thickens serve from the casserole.

Beefsteak en Casserole

Melt three tablespoons of butter, add six onions cut in slices and cook until light brown. Put the onions into the casserole, rinsing out the pan with a little hot water. Cut two pounds of beef cut from the top of the round into pieces for serving and sear in a hot omelet pan. Put into the casserole on top of the onions, with a sprig of parsley, salt and pepper and enough hot water to cover the onions. Cover and cook slowly for two hours or until nearly tender. Skim off the fat, add one cup of sliced potatoes which have been parboiled, and more seasonings if needed. Serve from casserole. —Stella A. Downing.

Casserole of Rice and Veal

The casserole of rice and veal makes a very appetizing as well as a sightly dish. Butter a melon mold with a brush, going into every crevice. Line the mold about three-quarters of an inch or one inch deep with the hot steamed rice. Prepare a mixture to fill the cavity, using two cups of finely chopped veal, seasoned very highly with salt, pepper, cayenne, celery salt, onion juice and lemon juice. Then add one-fourth cup of cracker crumbs, one egg slightly beaten, and enough hot stock to make it stick together. The mixture must not be too moist or too dry. Fill in the center of the mold with this, leaving about one inch at the top not filled. Into that put rice, smoothing it down, then put on the buttered lid of the mold and let it steam for forty-five minutes. Turn it out on a platter, garnish with parsley, and pour about it tomato sauce. This dish is very nice made with

cold mutton and is an excellent method
for using any meat left over; lamb,
chicken, beef or turkey will do.—See
Page XXII.

Swedish Timbales

Sift three-fourths of a cup of flour,
half a teaspoon of salt and one teaspoon
of sugar. Gradually add half a cup of
milk and one beaten egg, then one tablespoon of olive oil. Fry on a hot timbale
iron in deep fat till crisp and brown.
Take from the iron, invert on brown
paper to drain, then fill with any creamed
mixture of meat, chicken or fish. Serve
as an entree.—See Page XXV.

Chicken a la Providence

Thoroughly clean a chicken, truss it
neatly and firmly. For this, two skewers
are run through the upper and lower
parts of the legs, one through the wings,
then around it is wound string to keep
the fowl in shape. After trussing, salt
and pepper and place in a steamer to
cook for about an hour and a quarter.
Remove from the steamer, place it on a
hot platter, take out the skewers and
pour around the chicken a hot sauce
made by the following recipe:

Two cups of stock from the kettle
under the steamer are thickened with
two tablespoons of flour and two tablespoons of butter, cooked together. To
this are added, just before serving, half
a cup of carrot cut into very small cubes,
half a cup of peas, salt and pepper, the
yolks of two eggs and one teaspoon of
lemon juice.

After pouring the sauce around the
chicken, sprinkle the whole with finely
chopped parsley and serve.—See Page
XXVIII.

Sausages and Potatoes

One may easily transform a homely
platter of sausages into a most sightly
dish. Prepare plenty of mashed potato,
pressing it through a ricer, adding butter,

milk and seasoning, then whipping it
till light with a fork.   Make a bank of
the potato in the center of a platter and
around it build a wall of potato roses,
squeezed through a pastry bag.   Set this
in the oven to brown lightly.   Fry the
sausages, pricking them all over to prevent bursting.   When the skins are well
crisped lay a row of the sausages on the
bank of potato and send to the table
piping hot.—See Page XXVI.

Fillet of Chicken Broiled

From the breast of a chicken cut the
four fillets, which can be easily separated,
and remove every particle of fat or skin.
Dust lightly with salt.   Butter a piece of
heavy white letter paper and wrap it
lightly about the meat.   Lay on a broiler
over a clear fire and move constantly
over the heat.   The paper will brown and
gradually char, but before it takes fire—
you must lift it from the fire just before
this happens—you will find the fillet
nicely cooked and much less dry than if
cooked directly over the coals.—E. M. K.

Broiled Beef Balls

With a knife, scrape from a piece of
raw round steak as much as possible of
the soft part of the meat.   Dust with a
very little salt and form into balls in the
palm of the hand, but applying no more
pressure than absolutely necessary.   Cook
for two minutes on a hot omelet pan,
shaking the balls about so they will not
stick.—E. M. K.

Meat and Fish Sauces

Cucumber Cream Sauce

Chop one cucumber fine, season with one-half teaspoon of salt, one-half teaspoon each of chopped parsley and onion, one tablespoon of plain or tarragon vinegar or lemon juice. Mix thoroughly and let drain in a colander one-half hour. When ready to serve add three-fourths cup of cream beaten very stiff.—Stella A. Downing.

Bechamel Sauce

Cook one and a half cups of white stock twenty minutes with one slice of onion, one slice of carrot, a bit of bay leaf, a sprig of parsley and six peppercorns, then strain. It should be cooked down to about one cup of liquor. Melt four tablespoons of butter, four tablespoons of flour, and pour over it the hot sauce with one cup of scalded milk. Season with salt and pepper.—Stella A. Downing.

Sauce Tartare

Stir into a cup of mayonnaise, two small sweet-pickled cucumbers, three olives and a handful of watercress chopped fine; a few capers and a little onion juice. If you live in that happy valley where you can get a *fresh* shad for this course, by all means use it Broil it, garnish with quarters of lemon and with the roe, parboiled and broiled brown; rub with butter frequently while over the fire.—Anne Warner.

Shrimp Sauce

Pound one cup of shrimps, skins and all, in a mortar. Boil afterward for ten minutes in a cup of water. Press the liquor through a puree strainer. Mix one tablespoon of butter and one tablespoon of flour to a paste, pour over it the shrimp liquor. Season with salt, pap-

rika and one teaspoon of anchovy paste. Just before serving—and it must be served very hot—add half a dozen shrimps cut in inch pieces. This is one of the most delicious sauces that can accompany any fish.

Brown Sauce

Heat one cup of stock; blend together one tablespoon each of butter and flour, add to the hot stock with two cloves, one bay leaf, one teaspoon each of chopped onion and parsley. Cook for a few minutes. Strain and serve hot with cannelon of beef or rolled beef.—Stella A. Downing.

Drawn Butter Egg Sauce

Cook together, until well mixed, a tablespoon each of butter and flour. Add a cup of the water in which the fish boiled. Simmer five minutes, season highly with salt and mildly with pepper and serve in a tureen in which have been placed half a dozen slices of hard-boiled egg.

White Mushroom Sauce

Melt four tablespoons of butter, add one slice each of carrot and onion, a bit of bay leaf, sprig of parsley, six peppercorns, four tablespoons of flour, and slowly add two cups of white stock. Cook five minutes, remove seasonings and add one-half can of mushrooms cut in pieces and one-half teaspoon of lemon juice. Salt and pepper to taste.—Stella A. Downing.

Hollandaise Sauce

Cream half a cup of butter and add the yolks of two eggs one at a time, beating it thoroughly, then one-third of a cup of boiling water. Cook over a double boiler till it thickens to the consistency of a custard. The seasoning, which consists of one-fourth of a teaspoon of salt, a dash of cayenne and one tablespoon of lemon juice, is added just before the boiler is lifted from the fire.—Katherine A. French.

Sauce for Veal Cutlets

Two tablespoons of dripping, one-quarter cup of flour, one pint of stock or water and stock, one teaspoon or more of Worcestershire, two tablespoons of chopped parsley, one-half teaspoon of salt, one-eighth teaspoon of pepper. Prepare as a brown sauce, pour over cutlets and cook at low temperature for one hour, or until tender.—Mrs B. M. Chadbourn.

Pastry and Pies

Good Mincemeat Without Intoxicants

Five pounds of beef boiled until tender (it should be salted when partly done). Let cool in liquor, remove fat, chop very fine and measure. Use twice as much finely chopped apple, which should be tart, as meat. To the apple and meat then add the liquor in which the meat was boiled; also the fat which has been removed, and one quart of boiled cider. If there was a scant amount of fat, add also half a cup of butter. Jelly or candied fruit will improve the pies, if wanted richer. Add also three teaspoons of cloves, two of cinnamon, same of mace, and three pounds of seeded raisins. No definite rule can be given for sugar, as more or less is required, according to acidity of apples. Sweeten to taste with brown sugar. After all the ingredients have been put together, warm, and if found too thick for use, thin with cider or unfermented grape juice. When hot this can be put up as fruit and kept indefinitely.—Mrs E. M. Widdicomb.

Cream Pie

A cream pie without cream makes a dainty dessert. Line a deep plate with good paste, pricking it in several places with a fork to let the air out and prevent blisters, and bake a delicate brown. To make the filling, put over the fire in a double boiler one large cup of milk. Stir together half a cup of sugar, a piece of butter the size of a walnut, a small half cup of flour, one tablespoon of cold milk and the yolks of two well-beaten eggs. Mix until they are thoroughly blended, and add them to the milk when it boils. Stir until it thickens, and when the flour is cooked take from the fire and flavor with vanilla. Fill the crust that has been baked with custard, beat the whites

of the eggs to a froth, and add to them two tablespoons of powdered sugar; cover the top of the pie with them and brown lightly in the oven. The custard may be flavored with chocolate to make a change.

Lemon Pie

Four eggs, six tablespoons of sugar, five tablespoons of cold water, the grated rind and juice of one lemon, one tablespoon of melted butter, and a pinch of salt. Beat the yolks and sugar, stir in the rest and bake. Beat the whites sweetened, and spread over the top and brown slightly.—Mrs Whitney.

Apple Pie

Quarter and pare eight apples. Cut the quarters in two and fill a deep pie plate. If the apples are quite sour use two-thirds of a cup of granulated sugar; if only moderately so, half a cup. One teaspoon of cinnamon. Roll the under crust very thin. The upper crust should be punctured for the escape of the steam. After moistening the under crust around the edges fold the upper crust under it and press them together to keep in the juice. Bake in a moderate oven from half to three-quarters of an hour.

Pumpkin Pie

To make one pie, rub through a sieve cooked pumpkin enough to make two cups. To this add a small cup of sugar, a saltspoon of salt, one teaspoon of cinnamon and one of ginger and a pint of hot milk, and mix thoroughly. When cold stir in two well-beaten eggs and fill a pie plate that has been lined with good, rich paste. It will require three-quarters of an hour to bake.

Apple Custard Pie

Stew six large mealy apples, sweeten and flavor to taste. Take three eggs and separate the whites and yolks. Beat the yolks until light and add to the cooked

apples. Then beat the whole mixture, which should become very light. Line some pie tins with paste, pour in the mixture and set in the oven to bake. Beat the whites of the eggs to a stiff froth with sugar, flavor with vanilla or lemon. When the pie is baked, take it from the oven, spread the meringue on the top, and put back in the oven for a few moments until set and slightly browned. —Emelia Cowell.

Cheese Straws

Roll piecrust dough the same thickness as for pies. Cut in strips from six to ten inches wide and cut the strips into straws or sticks a quarter of an inch in width. Lay upon baking sheets, leaving a space between the straws a third the width of the straws. Grate rich cheese, season to taste with salt and red pepper and scatter thickly over the straws and the spaces between them. Put in the oven where the greatest heat will be at the top and bake ten or fifteen minutes. Cut the cheese in the center of the spaces between the straws, remove from the baking sheet with a limber knife and pile tastily on a plate.—Emma P. Ewing.

Lemon Pie with Raisins

One egg, one cup of raisins, one large lemon, one cup of boiling water, one cup of light brown sugar, half cup of molasses, two tablespoons of melted butter, one even tablespoon of flour. Chop raisins fine; grate the yellow part of lemon; stir the flour to a paste in cold water and add to the cup of boiling water. Beat the eggs and stir all together. This will make the filling for two pies with top and bottom crust.—Mrs S. Z. Foster.

Apple Pie with Pineapple

Bake an apple pie in the usual way, but without sweetening. While it is baking take three tablespoons of grated pineapple, one tablespoon of water, three of sugar, and simmer together till the

fruit looks clear. When the pie is taken from the oven, remove the top crust, spread the pineapple over the apple, replace the cover and set the pie away to cool. The pineapple mixture furnishes the sweetening.

Mince Pie

Ingredients: Four pounds of lean, cold boiled meat chopped fine, nine pounds of apples chopped fine, one and a half pounds of suet chopped fine, three pounds of raisins, two pounds of currants, half a pound of citron sliced fine, five pounds of sugar, three teaspoons of ground cloves, ten teaspoons of ground cinnamon, five teaspoons of ground mace, one teaspoon of ground black pepper, six tablespoons of salt, one quart of cider and vinegar mixed with one quart of molasses. Mix all, and add the juice and grated rind of two lemons; or, instead of cider, vinegar and molasses, one quart of sherry and one pint of brandy may be substituted. Keep this mincemeat in stone jars; add a little more liquor, if it should become too dry, when about to make pies.

Pie Crust

One-half cup of lard and one-half cup of butter. Work into three cups of flour. Moisten with cold water. Take half the quantity, roll to an inch in thickness. cover with small bits of butter, then form the whole into a roll. With a rolling-pin applied crosswise the roll, flatten it, and cover again with bits of butter. Repeat this operation three times, using in all about a quarter of a cup of butter. This is for the upper crust. The other half for the under crust needs to be rolled but once, and very thin for the pan. If to be filled with custard, squash, lemon or cream, bake the under crust first. To keep it smooth on the pan cut a piece of paper the size of the crust and partly fill it with flour. This flour can be used for gravies, etc. Of course the paper is to be removed before filling the

pie for the final baking. This will make four medium pies, both upper and under crust. This is much cheaper than puff paste and better for ordinary use.—Mrs E. C. Gardner.

Rissoles and Patty Cases

Rissoles are very dainty entrees, considered elaborate enough for the most formal occasion. Cut puff paste in oblong pieces three by four inches, or stamp out in rounds. Place a spoonful of any savory meat mixture (creamed chicken, sweetbreads or mushrooms, daintily seasoned, being most suitable) on the lower half, fold over the wet edges of upper half and press well together. A sauce is served with them. A satisfactory proportion is two tablespoons of butter, two tablespoons of flour, one cup of chicken or other stock. Study to season the mixtures and sauces in a way all your own, setting the seal of your own dainty individuality upon the dishes you prepare.

For patties, roll puff paste one-fourth inch thick, stamp out rounds with French cutter, remove centers from half the rounds, forming rings. Wet the edges of whole rounds, lay on the rings and press well together. Chill and bake twenty-five minutes.—See Page XVII.

A Pie Mold

In the "old country" where pastry is more hygienic than in America, it would be looked upon as deadly to eat a pie with a soaked under crust. Either there is no under crust, simply a well baked top and a filling of anything from pigeons to fruit, or a pie mold is made. For this purpose, puff paste may be used, or what the Scotch call "half puff," a pastry we would class as rich, with about half as much butter as flour. This paste is put on the outside of a bowl of tin or granite-ware, and pricked all over to keep it from puffing up in unseemly bubbles. A lid is fashioned from another round of pastry

covering a saucer. It is ornamented with medallions and scalloped edged ribbons of paste, put on according to the cook's taste. It must be very carefully baked and turned frequently. When cold slip it off the mold and serve in any way desired. It may hold creamed meat, any stewed fruit or fresh fruit with powdered sugar sifted over it.—See Page XXI.

Sandwiches and Canapes

Dream Cakes

Cut rounds or fancy shapes of crust-less bread. Spread first with a thin layer of American cheese, then with mayonnaise; or if preferred it may be dusted with cayenne pepper, and then put on bread; cover and fry in butter in chafing-dish.—Mrs S. F. Snow.

Onion Sandwiches

Cut bread very thin, removing all crust. Bermuda or Spanish onion chopped fine and mixed with rich mayonnaise dressing and spread between buttered bread. Sardines can also be added for a change.—Fanny M. Eby, Harrisburg.

Chicken and Celery Sandwiches

Put through the finest knife of the meat chopper one cup of cold chicken. Add to it one cup of celery cut very fine and four tablespoons of mayonnaise. Butter rounds of white bread, spread.

Salmon Sandwiches

Drain the oil from a can of salmon, remove the skin and bones and mash the fish very fine. Add to it the yolks of six hard-boiled eggs pressed through the potato ricer, half a teaspoon of salt, one-fourth teaspoon of paprika, two table-spoons of lemon juice, two tablespoons of chopped parsley and half a cup of boiled salad dressing. Spread between folds of white or entire wheat bread.

Caviar Canapes

Wash the contents of a can of Russian caviar long and thoroughly under running water. Drain and serve, seasoned highly with lemon juice and red pepper, in cups formed of halves of the whites of hard-boiled eggs. Set on rounds of delicately fried bread and press the yolks

through a sieve over the canapes after placing on the individual plates. Sardines, rubbed to a paste and a little parsley; or anchovies, with just a suspicion of mint, can be substituted for the caviar, if preferred.

A Brand New Sandwich

Chop two good-sized cucumbers fine, add a little onion juice, a dash of red pepper and mix with as much mayonnaise dressing. This filling is dainty and makes a very "tasty" sandwich.— Mrs E. H. Tichener.

A Club Sandwich

Toast a slice of bread evenly and lightly and butter it. On one half put, first, a thin slice of bacon which has been broiled till dry and tender, next a slice of the white meat of either turkey or chicken. Over one half of this place a circle cut from a ripe tomato and over the other half a tender leaf of lettuce. Cover these with a generous layer of mayonnaise, and complete this delicious "whole meal" sandwich with the remaining piece of toast.—A. W.

Mock Crab Sandwiches

To half a cup of grated cheese add four tablespoons of creamed butter, half a teaspoon each of salt, paprika and mustard, one teaspoon of anchovy paste and vinegar and two tablespoons of chopped olives. Spread between rounds of white bread.

Cheese Sandwiches

To half a cup of mild grated cheese and half a cup of Roquefort cheese rubbed to a paste, add one teaspoon of paprika and half a cup of cream. Beat till smooth and spread between graham bread.

Walnut and Cheese Sandwiches

Chop half a cup of walnut meats fine and mix with half a cup of Neufchatel cheese. Add a dash of pepper and salt if they seem to require seasoning. Spread

between slices of white bread. If desired this sandwich may be further improved by putting between the folds of a crisp lettuce leaf.

Anchovy Cheese Sandwiches

To one cottage cheese add two teaspoons of anchovy essence, one teaspoon of paprika and two tablespoons of chopped parsley. Spread between slices of entire wheat bread.

Dessert Sandwich

Cut sponge cake into thin oblongs or squares. Put between two pieces a slice of vanilla ice cream that has been molded in brick form. Ornament the top slice of cake with whipped cream (sweetened and flavored slightly with cordial) pressed through a pastry tube.—Anne Warner.

Toasted Sandwiches

Butter thin slices of bread as if preparing sandwiches and put them together. Trim off the crusts. Lay them in a wire broiler and hold over a clear fire till very delicately browned. Serve hot.

Canape Lorenzo

Chop a small shallot, fry lightly in two ounces of butter, without coloring. Add a tablespoon of flour wet with a pint of cream, then one pint of crab meat; salt and pepper to taste and leave on the fire till it bubbles. Cut slices of bread one-quarter of an inch thick, trim in any desired shape and toast on one side only. Put the mixture on the toasted side and cover one-eighth of an inch thick with butter prepared as follows: One-quarter of a pound of butter, one-half a pound of grated Parmesan cheese and a seasoning of both red and white pepper. Lay the canapes on a buttered dish and color in the oven.

Salads of Meat, Fish, Vegetables and Fruit

Fruit Salad

Blanch the meat of two dozen English walnuts and break in pieces. Skin and seed two dozen white grapes, cut one pineapple in slices and slices in cubes. Slice three bananas. Separate the sections of two large oranges and remove all skin. Arrange each in separate piles. Pour over a dressing made of one-half cup of Madeira wine, one cup of sugar, two tablespoons of lemon juice and one-half cup of orange juice. Garnish with Maraschino cherries.

Halibut Salad

Chop very fine one pound of cooked halibut, season with a few drops of onion juice, two teaspoons of lemon juice, one-half teaspoon of paprika, one and one-half teaspoons of salt and a few grains of cayenne; add one-third cup of thick cream, which has been beaten until stiff, and the whites of three well-beaten eggs. Cook in buttered timbale molds until firm. Chill, remove from pans, arrange on salad dish, garnish with mayonnaise around and on top of fish and shrimps at the base.—Maria Willett Howard.

No-name Salad

Make a mayonnaise, a small amount of aspic and a French dressing. Flake any cold cooked fish, either of one kind or mixed, and lay for an hour in a deep plate sprinkled with oil and vinegar. Line a plain, flat-topped mold with the just liquid aspic by pouring in a small quantity and turning and tipping the mold in a bed of cracked ice till every part is thickly coated; then set firmly and evenly in the ice. Ornament the bottom (which will be the top) with a round of

truffle in the center and a dozen or so
shrimps radiating from it, and decorate
the sides with a ring of shrimps alter-
nating with slices of truffle; set these
with a very little more aspic. Add to the
mayonnaise about its own bulk of the
jelly and put in the mold a layer of the
mixture, then one of the fish just as you
lift it from the marinade; strew with
capers, add another layer of sauce, then
fish, till the mold is full; garnish with a
wreath of cauliflower branches and water
cress well seasoned with the French
dressing when turned out for the table.—
Anne Warner.

Salmon Salad

Place on a bed of lettuce leaves, in a
flat salad bowl, the contents of half a
can of salmon, freed from oil and bones,
and flaked. Pour over the fish a little
boiled salad dressing or mayonnaise, and
garnish with slices of hard-boiled eggs
and lemon.

Garcia Salad

Cut celery, apples and fresh tomatoes
in thin strips about two inches long, serve
on lettuce leaves with French dressing.
A slice of truffle on the top adds to the
appearance and flavor.

Bavarian Salad

Shred very fine two heads of lettuce,
chop two onions fine and cut one cold
beet into cubes. Make a layer of the
lettuce, toss together the beets and onion
and pile on the lettuce. Marinate with a
French dressing, pour over the top an
oil mayonnaise and garnish with sliced
olives.

Potato Pepper Salad

Cut three large cold potatoes into half-
inch dice. Remove the seeds from a
green pepper and chop it fine. Mix four
tablespoons of vinegar with two tablespoons of ice water, one-fourth teaspoon
of powdered sugar, a dash of pepper and
half a teaspoon of salt. Put a layer of

potatoes in the salad dish, then a layer
of the chopped pepper and sprinkle over
it a tablespoon of oil. Put in another
layer of potatoes and peppers, add another tablespoon of oil, then pour over
all the vinegar. Set in the refrigerator
for fifteen minutes to marinate.—Maria
Willett Howard.

Grand Union Cabbage

Select a small, heavy cabbage and roll
back the outside leaves. Cut out the
center, leaving the shell entire. With a
sharp knife slice the heart of the cabbage very thin and soak in ice water till
crisp. Drain and dry between towels.
Add two green peppers cut in fine strips
and mix with a French dressing. For
this use half a teaspoon of salt, a quarter
teaspoon of pepper, one tablespoon of
vinegar and four tablespoons of salad
oil. Stir till well blended pour over the
cabbage and peppers, then refill the bowl.
—Stella A. Downing.

Grape Fruit Salad

Peel the fruit, separate the sections,
remove the skin and take out the seeds.
Blanch Malaga grapes by throwing into
hot water for a minute, cut in two and
remove the seeds. Mix with the grape
fruit and serve with mayonnaise. Garnish with lettuce and celery.—Mrs Cor-
nelius Stevenson, Philadelphia.

English Walnut and Chicken Salad

For this salad there will be required
twenty-four English walnuts, onion,
parsley, chicken liquor, celery, cold
cooked chicken, French dressing and
mayonnaise dressing. Take one pint of
the chicken cut into dice one pint of
celery cut into dice, and parboil the English walnuts long enough to remove the
skins. In boiling the nuts, add a slice
of onion, a sprig of parsley and a little
chicken liquor, then drain, remove the
brown skins and mix them with the celery
and chicken. Pour over this a cup of

French dressing and put in the refrigerator for an hour or more. At serving time, stir half a pint of mayonnaise dressing into this. Make shells of crisp lettuce leaves, put a tablespoon of salad in each and a teaspoon of the mayonnaise on top, and serve.—Ella E. Woodbridge

White Grape Salad

One pound of white grapes, one head of lettuce, one pint of chopped celery, mayonnaise dressing. Cut grapes in two, taking out seeds, or skin grapes if you desire. For mayonnaise take yolks of two eggs, beat three minutes with Dover egg beater. Add oil gradually, about a cup. When thick add one teaspoon of salt, one-half teaspoon of sugar, the juice of half a lemon, or a tablespoon of vinegar, and a dash of red pepper. Keep all ingredients perfectly cold. When ready to serve, mix mayonnaise dressing, celery and grapes, and send to the table on lettuce leaves.—Mrs Joshua L. Miner, Wilkesbarre.

Cabbage Salad

Chop cabbage to make three pints, add two tablespoons of sugar and one tablespoon of salt. Boil one cup of vinegar, add a heaping tablespoon of butter, then add slowly two well-beaten eggs, then the chopped cabbage. Stir well, remove from the fire and cool. If desired, one-half cup of sweet cream may be added. Serve with lettuce or in cups made from hollowed peppers, tomatoes or cooked beets.

Waldorf Salaa

Two cups of celery chopped fine, grated rind of one orange, one cup of apples cut in dice. If fine red apples take six and scoop out insides, making little cups for the salads. Mix the above with the following mayonnaise: One very cold egg yolk with one teaspoon of onion juice and yolk of one boiled egg,

one cup of cold olive oil, one tablespoon of sugar, one tablespoon of vinegar, one tablespoon of lemon juice, one teaspoon of salt, one-fourth teaspoon of cayenne, one-half teaspoon of mustard. Mix thoroughly by stirring oil, drop by drop, to the egg and a few drops of vinegar, lemon, salt, pepper, etc, which have been previously thoroughly mixed together; then fill the cups or make plain mixture, serving on white lettuce leaves. Cheese balls are delicious served with this salad. —Mrs Howard P. Denison.

French Dressing

One and one-half teaspoons of salt, one-quarter teaspoon of pepper, six table-spoons of olive oil, two tablespoons of vinegar, cayenne, onion juice. Rub the bowl with an onion or use three drops of onion juice; add salt and pepper, olive oil and vinegar, and stir for five minutes with a piece of ice, remove ice, and beat until quite thick, keep in a cool place until ready to serve

Mayonnaise Dressing

One egg yolk, one cup of olive oil, one and one-half teaspoons of salt, one-quarter teaspoon of cayenne, one and one-half teaspoons of mustard, one table-spoon of lemon juice, one tablespoon of vinegar Mix in a cold bowl mustard, salt, pepper, yolk of egg and lemon juice, stir well, then add oil drop by drop; as mixture thickens thin with vinegar, keep in cold place until ready to serve. If a thinner dress-ing is liked, add one-half cup of beaten cream to the above mixture. If dressing is to be kept for any length of time use the yolk of a hard-boiled egg in addition to the raw yolk.

Boiled Salad Dressing

One and one-half teaspoons of mus-tard, one and one-half teaspoons of salt, two teaspoons of flour, one-half teaspoon of paprika, one-eighth teaspoon of cay-enne, one and one-half teaspoons of

melted butter, two egg yolks, one-quarter cup of vinegar. Mix ingredients in order given in the top of a double boiler, cook over hot water, until thick like soft custard, pour immediately into cold bowl and add one-half cup of cream which has been beaten until stiff.

Simple Salad Dressing

Two teaspoons of mustard, one and one-half teaspoons of salt, one-eighth teaspoon of cayenne, four eggs, one-half cup of vinegar, one-quarter cup of olive oil. Mix mustard, salt and cayenne, add eggs well beaten. Heat vinegar and oil in the top of the double boiler, when hot pour on to egg mixture, return to double boiler and cook until mixture thickens. Cool and keep in a covered jar; this dressing will keep for weeks. —Maria Willett Howard.

Fruit Salad (for twelve)

Six mellow sour apples, cut into dice. Six oranges, pulp separated from inner skin, half a pound of blanched almonds cut fine with knite, dice cut from candied pineapple. Garnish with half walnuts and candied cherries. Serve on the inner leaves of crisp head lettuce, with a heaping spoon of mayonnaise dressing, or two spoons of French dressing, added just before serving.—Mrs Thomas K. Gray.

Egg and Lobster Salad

Cook one dozen eggs, remove shells, cut a small piece from the top and a slice from the bottom of each, the latter to make them stand, remove yolks, fill the whites with lobster, celery and cucumber, all cut fine, and mixed with mayonnaise dressing. Serve one of these to each person upon plates of lettuce garnished with the yolks highly seasoned and made into tiny balls. A French dressing should be poured over the lettuce. Serve with this snowballs made ot cream cheese and whipped cream, mashed smooth, and long strips of puiled bread, browned and hot. The eggs should be

put in boiling water, which should not boil after eggs are in. Leave them in this bath thirty-five minutes.—Linda Hull Larned

Spanish Salad

One cup of chicken meat cut in small pieces, cucumber cut in cubes, one cup of English walnut meats broken in pieces, one-half can of French peas and two cups of celery cut in strips, well mixed with a silver fork; add one cup of simple salad dressing. Serve very cold on shredded lettuce or individually in lettuce nests, and garnish with Spanish peppers cut in points.

Tomato and Mushroom Salad

Scoop out six tomatoes, leaving a shell, mix the pulp with an equal quantity of chopped olives and chopped mushrooms, allow two tablespoons of French dressing to each tomato, refill tomato shells, garnish with mayonnaise dressing, and serve on lettuce or watercress.

Blood Orange Salad

Take the pulp from eight blood oranges, add one cup of Wiesbaden strawberries, the pulp of one grape fruit, one banana delicately sliced, and serve with the fruit syrup.

Neufchatel Salad

Mash two rolls of Neufchatel cheese, add two tablespoons of finely chopped olives, moisten with cream, season with salt and cayenne, form into small balls. Marinate with a French dressing. Serve on shredded lettuce and garnish with four red peppers cut in strips, and arranged in four piles in star shape.

Orange Salad

Select Jamaica or Messina oranges of uniform size and small, cut in thin slices and slices in quarters. Marinate with one-third cup of olive oil, two tablespoons of lemon juice, six drops of tabasco sauce, one-half teaspoon of salt

and one teaspoon of paprika mixed together. Serve on a bed of watercress. —Maria Willett Howard.

Orange and Banana Salad

Cut four large oranges in halves and scoop out the pulp, add to this four bananas cut in dice, pour over it the fruit syrup.

Pineapple and Banana Salad

Use home-canned pineapple which has been cooked in the jars, or the market variety of pineapple which comes very slightly sweetened in large cans holding entire slices of the fruit. Cut the pineapple into small dice and drain away the juice. To one cup of pineapple dice add one cup of finely sliced banana and pour over a syrup flavored with Maraschino. Serve in lemon cups.

Apple and Orange Salad

Fine juicy apples with a slightly acid flavor, cut in dice and mingled with orange pulp, make a delicious salad. Add half a cup of Maraschino cherries.

Cauliflower Salad

Stand a firm white cauliflower in salt water for half an hour, then cook it in boiling water until tender but not quite done. Drain, cool, cut into sprigs and arrange these neatly in a salad bowl lined with tender leaves. Mash the yolks of four hard-boiled eggs and cut the whites into petals, arrange these like daisies over the cauliflower and pour over a plain French dressing. Serve very cold. —Mary Foster Snider.

Summer Salad

Select six fresh cucumbers all the same size. Pare, cut in halves lengthwise, scoop out the centers and lay in water till wanted. Dry and fill with a mixture of sweetbreads and peas, dressed with mayonnaise. Set on a green lettuce leaf on individual plates. Serve with dainty plain bread and butter sandwiches.— Anne Warner.

Cherry Salad

Stone half a pound of cherries and save all the juice. Take the whitest leaves of a nice head of lettuce and wash them thoroughly. Slice a small cucumber and chop fine a dozen blanched almonds. Mix all gently together, arrange on the lettuce leaves, and pour over a dressing made of a gill of cherry juice, two tablespoons of lemon juice, a drop or two of almond extract and four tablespoons of sugar. Serve very cold.—Mary F. Snider.

Spinach Salad

Pick over, wash and cook one-half peck of spinach. Drain and chop fine. Season with salt, pepper and lemon juice and add one tablespoon of melted butter. Butter small tin molds slightly and pack solidly with the mixture. Chill, remove from mold and arrange on thin slices of cold boiled tongue, cut in circular pieces. Garnish base of each with parsley and serve on top of each sauce tartare.—Stella A. Downing.

Strawberry Salad

Arrange large ripe strawberries in a glass salad bowl, dust with powdered sugar and a little nutmeg. Pour over a dressing made of two tablespoons of sugar, a gill of sherry, a tablespoon of Maraschino, the juice of one lemon and two oranges; mix the fruit light with a fork and set on ice half an hour before serving.

Macedoine Salad

Cut into neat cubes one cold beet, one cold carrot, two cold potatoes and one cup of cold string beans. Put each vegetable separately into a sauce dish and marinate with a French dressing for a half hour, setting it in the refrigerator. Serve arranged in small spoonfuls on individual lettuce leaves with a light mask of mayonnaise on each one and whole string beans as a garnish.

Tomato and Hickory Nut Salad

Dissolve a box of acidulated gelatine in cold water enough to cover it, using the pink powder inclosed in the gelatine. Rub the tomatoes through a sieve, add salt and a pinch of red pepper and the dissolved gelatine, and after heating thoroughly and cooling add chopped hickory nuts and small pieces of celery. Set to cool in a mold. Stir occasionally until it begins to set. When ready to serve, cover with the following dressing: One teaspoon of salt, one teaspoon of sugar, one teaspoon of mustard and three tablespoons of vinegar. Stir in three eggs, one at a time; mix thoroughly. Cook in a double boiler. When cool mix in a pint of stiffly whipped cream and pour over the molded tomato and scatter chopped nuts over it. When serving have a dish filled with crisp, curly lettuce leaves beside your salad, put a leaf on the plate, then a spoon of salad and proceed to eat.—Mrs D. L. Bardwell.

Japanese Salad

Wash even-sized beets and cook them in boiling salted water until tender—an hour or longer. Plunge them into cold water and rub off the skin. With a sharp knife and a spoon remove the center from each beet, leaving a cup. Let them stand in weak vinegar on ice. Cut into dice enough cold boiled potato to make two cups, add one cup of diced celery, one tablespoon of chopped parsley, a few drops of onion juice and one tablespoon of pecan nut meats. Mix all lightly with a fork, marinate with French dressing made with one-half teaspoon of salt, one-fourth teaspoon of paprika, three tablespoons of olive oil and one tablespoon of vinegar or lemon juice. When ready to serve, arrange nests of lettuce leaves on a platter, dry the beet cups, fill them with the salad and place a beet in each nest of leaves,

putting a teaspoon of mayonnaise on top of each cup just before serving.

Mayonnaise: Mix together one teaspoon each of dry mustard, powdered sugar and salt, and a little cayenne. Add the yolks of two eggs, beating well with a wooden spoon. Add gradually, a few drops at a time, one pint of olive oil; thin with two tablespoons of lemon juice added alternately, a little at a time, with the oil. Last of all, add two tablespoons of vinegar gradually. This dressing should be mixed in a saucepan set in ice water.—Annabel Lee.

Sweetbread Salad

Soak one pair of sweetbreads in cold water for twenty minutes, then cook in boiling salted water twelve minutes. Cool and cut in slices, mix with one cup of celery cut in small pieces, cover with French dressing and chill for at least one-half hour. Serve in nests made of the crisp inner leaves of a head of lettuce, and garnish with one cup of mayonnaise dressing.

Tomato Jelly

Cook two cups of tomatoes with one slice of onion, one teaspoon of salt and one-eighth teaspoon of pepper twenty minutes, strain; add two tablespoons of granulated gelatine which has been soaked in one-quarter cup of cold water, and stir until gelatine is dissolved, pour into a border mold which has been previously dipped in cold water.—Maria Willett Howard.

Potato Salad

Cut cold boiled potatoes into even dice (about six potatoes). Mix with these the chopped whites of three hard-boiled eggs. Mix the yolks with a scant teaspoon of dry mustard and stir into it a large cup of thick sour cream; add a little paprika, pour the dressing over the potato and mix gently. This is very delicious. No salt is needed if the pota-

toes are boiled with a pinch of salt in the water.—Mrs Clinton Locke, Chicago.

Celery Salad

Cut the tender stalks of celery into inch pieces to make three cups, marinate with a French dressing. Serve in a ring of tomato jelly, and garnish with curled celery, shredded lettuce and mayonnaise dressing.

Shellfish

Lobster Cutlets

Two cups of lobster meat, two tablespoons of flour, one tablespoon of
chopped parsley, three-fourths of a
cup of cream or milk, one tablespoon
of butter, two eggs (yolks only).
Chop the fish into small pieces, using
a silver knife, and adding the seasoning. Heat the milk to scalding, rub
the butter and flour to a smooth paste,
add this to the milk and stir until it
thickens. Then add the beaten yolks of
the eggs. Cook one minute and remove
from the fire. Carefully add the lobster
to this mixture and set aside to cool.
When cold form into balls, dip first into
beaten egg and then in bread or cracker
dust and fry in smoking hot fat. Drain
upon soft brown paper and serve garnished with lemon.

Clams Cooked with Cream

Chop fifty small clams not too fine and
season them with pepper and salt. Put
into a stewpan butter the size of an
egg, and when it bubbles sprinkle in a
teaspoon of flour, which cook a few
moments; stir gradually into it the clam
liquor, then the clams, which stew about
two or three minutes; then add a cup
of boiling cream and serve immediately.
The clams may or may not be breaded.

Baked Clams

Prepare twenty-five clams and drain.
Take one-half pint of cracker crumbs,
one-half cup of warm milk, one-fourth
cup of clam liquor, two beaten eggs, one
heaping tablespoon of butter, and salt
and pepper. Mix in one dish the
crackers, and moisten first with the milk,
then with clam liquor. Add the eggs
and butter and the clams chopped fine.
Fill twelve clam shells heaping full,

sprinkle each with bread crumbs and brown in the oven.—Mrs A. B. Brown.

Clam Fritters

Strain one pint of clams, saving the juice; add to this juice sufficient water to make one pint; mix into it one egg, well beaten, and sufficient prepared flour to make a light batter, also the clams chopped and some salt. Drop by the spoonful into boiling hot lard.

Oyster Cocktail

Mix together the strained juice of half a lemon, one-half teaspoon of vinegar, eight drops of tabasco sauce, one-half teaspoon of horse-radish and one-half teaspoon of tomato catsup. Add eight oysters and let stand five minutes. Do not chop large oysters, but use blue points or a small oyster. Have glasses chilled before filling. Use claret or cocktail glasses.—Mrs J. T. Baxter.

Lobster Wiggle

Into the chafing-dish put two table-spoons of butter and two tablespoons of flour. Stir together till like a paste, add one cup of cream or rich milk, half a teaspoon of salt, a dash of paprika, one teaspoon of lemon juice and chopped parsley. Beat till creamy with a whisk, add one and one-half cups of lobster meat cut into small cubes Cook for a few minutes with the lid on. Just before serving add half a can of French peas. Pour over fingers of buttered toast.

Soft Shell Crabs

Dry the crabs, sprinkle them with pepper and salt; roll them, first in flour, then in egg (half a cup of milk mixed in one egg), then in cracker dust, and fry them in boiling lard.

Deviled Crab

When the crabs are boiled, take out the meat and cut it into small pieces; clean well the shells. To six ounces of crab meat mix two ounces of bread crumbs, two hard-boiled eggs chopped,

the juice of half a lemon, cayenne pepper
and salt. Mix all with cream or cream
sauce, or, what is still better, a Bechamel
sauce. Fill the shells with the mixture,
smooth the tops, sprinkle over sifted
bread crumbs, and color in a quick oven.

Oyster Cocktail

Seven teaspoons of horse-radish, seven
teaspoons of vinegar, ten teaspoons of
lemon juice, one teaspoon of tabasco
sauce, salt to taste, one quart of oysters
for twelve people. Serve in glasses.—
Mrs L. M. Powers.

Lobster Thackeray

Two or three lobsters cut into squares,
the fat (or green part) of one or two,
one saltspoon of salt, three dashes of red
pepper, one tablespoon of walnut catsup;
one-fourth pound of butter, one scant
spoon of paprika. This can be made in
a chafing-dish.—Mrs Samuel Adler.

Stuffed Lobster a la Merinole

A boiled lobster cut in half lengthwise; cut meat in small pieces, use the
coral if any; chop an onion fine, put in
saucepan with lump of butter; when
brown add lobster meat, a pinch of curry
powder, a pinch of English mustard, a
few pieces of celery cut small. Let this
cook for a few minutes, then add cup of
cream, cook in double boiler until thick;
then add three egg yolks and when cold
fill lobster shell. Take grated cheese
and bread crumbs and drawn butter and
pour over the top. Brown in oven for
from five to eight minutes.—Mrs David
Friend.

Crab Ravigote

Boil some large hardshell crabs, after
which put them aside to become cold.
Then turn them over on the hardshell
side and with a sharp knife cut the breast
away. Pick the meat off, clean it nicely,
being careful not to leave any pieces of
shell in it, and season lightly with salt
and pepper. Mix with thick remoulade

sauce and fill up one of the shells, which
has previously been washed clean, with
the mixture. The meat of two good sized
crabs so treated will be sufficient to fill
the inside of one shell. Cover the meat
with   mayonnaise   and   decorate   with
fillet of anchovy and sliced pickles.
Serve on a folded napkin with branches
of parsley and quartered lemon. ("Os-
car").—Mrs D. Webster Dougherty,
Philadelphia.

Oyster Loaf

Prepare a fresh loaf of baker's bread
by cutting out a square from one end
and tearing out the inside, as whole as
possible. When but a shell is left, butter
it well inside. Wash and drain a quantity of fine oysters, according to the size
of the loaf, and fill it exactly as you
would a dish for scalloped oysters, seasoning in layers with butter, pepper and
salt, but omitting the crumbs. Replace
the end of the loaf, rub the outside
lightly with butter, set in a dripping pan
and bake for about half an hour—a little
longer than in a dish. The loaf will
swell enough to keep the "lid" in place.
Serve on a long platter in a border of
cress. Probably as you try to cut it, it
will crush to a savory mass.   Make
pulled bread of the inside of the loaf and
dry in the oven.—Anne Warner.

Scalloped Scallops

Fry a light brown in butter, shaking
often to prevent burning; if you have
the shells, wash thoroughly and butter;
otherwise use a baking dish well buttered; put in a layer of bread crumbs,
well buttered, then one of scallops, and
so on until the dish is full, having the
crumbs at the top; cover with a white
sauce made of two tablespoons of butter
and two tablespoons of flour cooked
together and then stirred smooth in a
pint of milk, and bake twenty minutes,
or until nicely browned.

Fricassee of Oysters

Put one quart, or twenty-five, oysters on the fire in their own liquor. The moment it begins to boil, turn it into a hot dish through a colander, leaving the oysters in the colander. Put into the saucepan two ounces of butter (size of an egg) and when it bubbles sprinkle in one ounce (a tablespoon) of sifted flour; let it cook a minute without taking color, stirring it well with a wire egg-whisk; then add, mixing well, a cup of oyster liquor. Take it from the fire and mix in the yolks of two eggs, a little salt, a very little cayenne pepper, one teaspoon of lemon juice, and one grating of nutmeg. Beat it well; then return it to the fire to set the eggs, without allowing it to boil. Put in the oysters. These oysters may be served on thin slices of toast for breakfast or tea, or in papers, or as a filling for patties for dinner.

One Way to Prepare a Lobster

Put into a saucepan butter the size of a small egg, and one teaspoon of minced onion. When it has cooked, sprinkle in one teaspoon of flour, which cook also; then stir in one cup of the water in which the lobster was boiled, one cup of milk, one cup of strong veal or beef stock, pepper and salt. Add the meat of the boiled lobster, and when quite hot pour all in the center of a hot platter. Decorate the dish with the lobster's head in the center, fried bread diamonds (croutons) around the outside; or with the abundant resources of lobster legs and trimmings.—Mrs E. C. Gardner.

Scalloped Lobster

Remove the meat from a two-pound lobster and cut in cubes. Make one and one-half cups of white sauce by melting three tablespoons of butter, add four and one-half tablespoons of flour, one and one-half cups of milk, one-half teaspoon of salt, one-eighth teaspoon of pepper.

Cook until thick. Add the lobster meat, a few grains of cayenne, two teaspoons of lemon juice. Refill the shells, cover with buttered crumbs and bake until crumbs are brown.

Panned Oysters

Wash the oysters. Take one-half cup of butter and brown it. Cook the oysters in the butter. Beat the yolks of two eggs, add half a cup of milk and half a tablespoon of cornstarch. Mix all together, let come to a boil, and pour over toast for serving. This is for one can of oysters.—Mrs S. M. Jones.

Club House Oysters

Three tablespoons of butter, four tablespoons of flour, one and one-half teaspoons of mustard, one-half teaspoon of paprika, one teaspoon of parsley, one teaspoon of salt, one and one-half cups of oyster liquid, two tablespoons of lemon juice, two tablespoons of Worcestershire sauce, one pint of oysters. Melt butter, add other ingredients in order given and cook until oysters are plump. Serve on hot buttered toast with pimolas. If a more highly seasoned dish is desired, soak the oysters in French dressing for half an hour before cooking.

Creamed Oysters with Celery

Clean one pint of oysters and cook them in their own liquor until they are plump. Drain, then strain the oyster liquor and add to it enough thin cream to make one and a half cups. Melt in the chafing-dish three tablespoons of butter, add five tablespoons of flour and stir to a paste. Pour in the liquid gradually, and beat till creamy. Season with pepper, salt and celery salt. Add the parboiled oysters and cook till just at the boiling point. This may be poured over slices of buttered toast, then sprinkle with very finely chopped celery. If plain creamed oysters are desired, leave out the celery and celery salt, and if toast

is not obtainable, the dish is excellent served with bread and butter sandwiches. —I. G. C.

Cream Crab

One tablespoon of butter, three table-spoons of flour, one teaspoon of minced onion, one blade of mace, salt and pepper; meat of one crab in rather large pieces; one pint of cream; one egg beaten. Cook onion and mace in the butter. Take spoon and remove onion and mace. Add the flour and cook a minute. Then add cream and cook until it thickens. Season. Add beaten egg and then the crab. When crab is hot, serve on toast.—Mrs D. A. Lindley, Sacramento, Cal.

Shrimps, Newburg Style

These are prepared in the chafing-dish. Use the shrimps which come in glass. Melt a tablespoon of butter, add the contents of two jars of shrimps, which have been drained and wiped dry, season with a teaspoon of salt and a dash of cayenne, one tablespoon of brandy and two of sherry; cover and cook slowly five minutes. In the meantime, beat the yolks of four eggs thoroughly and add one cup of cream to them. Pour over the shrimps, stir a few moments till creamy and serve immediately, with the celery and home-made finger rolls.

Broiled Lobster

Only live lobsters are cooked in this way. Kill the fish by inserting a sharp knife in its back between the body and tail shells, severing the spinal cord. Split the shell the entire length of the back, remove the stomach and intestinal canal, crack the large claws, and lay the fish as flat as possible. Brush the meat with melted butter, season with salt and pepper, place in a broiler, and with the flesh side down, broil slowly until a delicate brown, twenty minutes usually sufficing. Turn the broiler, and broil for ten minutes longer. By covering the broiler with

an inverted roasting pan the heat will be more concentrated. Serve hot, passing melted butter with the lobster.

Oysters Grilled in the Chafing-dish

Wash a pint of large oysters, pick them from the liquor and drain as dry as possible. Put them in a well-heated blazer and as fast as liquor drains from them, remove it with a spoon. When the oysters are dry and plump they are ready to serve. Before taking from the pan, dust with pepper and salt and add two tablespoons of butter. Serve between saltine wafers sandwich fashion.— I. G. C.

Escalloped Oysters

One pint of oysters, two tablespoons of butter, two tablespoons of cream, salt and pepper, two tablespoons of oyster liquor. Pick crumbs from a slice of bread. Put in bottom of baking dish first a thick layer of crumbs, then a layer of oysters with the cream and liquor, then a layer of crumbs, and a little melted butter. Bake twenty-five minutes in center grate of oven.—Mrs H. C. Stimpson.

Oysters a la Snowdon (for chafing-dish)

Heat one quart of cream, seasoned to taste with celery salt, paprika and a few drops of tabasco. When very hot place in cream about a pint and a half of large selected oysters, thoroughly drained, and let stand until a trifle curled. Then add two or three tablespoons of Madeira and serve in hot plates.—Mrs Walter Snowdon Smith.

A Little Oyster Stew

Put into the chafing-dish two tablespoons of butter and one tablespoon of flour. Stir with a whisk till like a paste, then pour in one cup of strained oyster liquid and four tablespoons of cream. When it begins to boil add twenty oysters and a dust of paprika and salt. Put on the lid and allow the stew to cook for about two minutes. Then the gills will

be curled up. Serve in bouillon cups
with saltine wafers.

Deviled Oysters

Clean, drain and slightly chop one pint
of oysters. Add to a sauce made from
four tablespoons of butter, four tablespoons of flour and two-thirds of a cup
of scalded milk. Add the yolk of one
egg, half a teaspoon of salt, a dash of
cayenne, one teaspoon of lemon juice and
half a tablespoon of finely chopped
parsley. Arrange buttered oyster shells
in a dripping pan, half fill with the mixture and cover with buttered crumbs.
Bake from twelve to fifteen minutes in a
hot oven. Send to the table garnished
with parsley and lemon points.— See
Page XVIII.

Lobster Cream

Chop the meat of a two-pound lobster
fine. Cook half a cup of stale bread
crumbs in half a cup of milk for ten
minutes. Add to this a fourth of a cup
of cream, two teaspoons of anchovy essence, half a teaspoon of salt, a few
grains of cayenne and the whites of three
eggs beaten stiff. Turn into a buttered
oval mold, set in a pan of hot water,
cover the top of the dish with buttered
paper and bake twenty minutes in a
moderate oven.—See Page XXVII.

Soups

Clear Soups

Take strong, well flavored stock, and clear it. For "additions," each of which gives its name to the soup, a great many things may be used, as the various soup balls, rice, noodles, macaroni, poached eggs, cheese (grated), spaghetti, vermicelli (to any of which chopped parsley may be effectively added), and almost any vegetable, diced, chopped or grated in strings, and then cooked.—E. M. K.

Consomme

This is a specially fine recipe, and is not given in any cook book. Put two pounds of perfectly lean round steak in a hot frying pan, and let it cook quickly to a deep brown on both sides; when so browned chop fine, cover with two quarts of cold, strong, highly flavored stock. add the half-beaten whites and crushed shells of two eggs, beat well and proceed as in clearing soup. When strained, it is ready for reheating and serving.— E. M. K.

Quickly Made Beef Tea

Pour three-quarters of a cup of cold water over half a pound of raw hamburg steak. Allow it to stand ten minutes in a cool place, then set on the stove and let it cook slowly for ten minutes. Add a little salt, just before taking from the fire, and strain.

Chicken Broth

Use the legs of a chicken for this dish. Break the joints and cut up the meat into small strips. Pour over it four cups of water, add one tablespoon of rice and half a teaspoon of salt, then allow it to simmer very slowly for an hour and a half. Strain out the rice and meat and cool. Skim off the fat and reheat as

much of the broth as is required. In hot weather the rice may sour the broth, so make without and keep the soup in a tightly corked jar in the refrigerator.— E. M. K.

Clam Chowder

Two dozen clams, three-quarters pound of lean pork, three onions of medium size, one pint of tomatoes, celery to flavor, potatoes to thicken (about one quart), one pint of milk. Chop pork and brown in an iron kettle very brown. Then put in the water and other ingredients except milk. Cook one hour, then put in the milk just before removing from the fire.—Mrs S. F. Snow.

Fish Chowder

One pound of cod or haddock, four small potatoes, one small onion, one thin slice of fat salt pork, one cup of milk and one cup of fish stock, two tablespoons of flour, salt and pepper for seasoning. Place the bones, after removing them from the fish, in cold water, allowing it to heat gradually. Scald the potatoes, sliced thin, in boiling water for five minutes. Cut the pork in half inch cubes and try out the fat. Add the onions and heat in the fat. Then remove the pieces of pork and add the potatoes and the fish cut in medium-sized pieces. Dredge with flour and seasoning and then strain the fish stock over. Cook until the potatoes are done and the fish is tender, adding hot water if it is needed during the cooking. Add the milk, reheat and season again if necessary. Serve hot.

Hasty Tomato Soup

Boil one quart of milk, and add one cup of canned or cooked tomatoes, also cracker or bread crumbs to thicken sufficiently. Season with butter, pepper and salt, bring to a boil and serve.—Sarah M. Siewer, M D.

Cream of Lima Bean Soup

Soak one cup of dried beans over night, in the morning drain and add three

pints of cold water. Cook till soft and rub through a sieve. Cut two slices of onion and four slices of carrot in cubes and cook five minutes in two tablespoons of butter. Remove the vegetables, add two tablespoons of flour, one teaspoon of salt and half a teaspoon of pepper, stir into the boiling soup. Just before straining into the tureen add one cup of cream.

Potato Soup

Eight large potatoes, one large onion, one-half pound of salt pork cut into strips, three whole cloves and one sprig of parsley. Boil all two hours, then strain through a sieve and season to taste, adding one tablespoon of butter and one pint of cream. Let it come to a boil and serve.—Mrs Frank Rockefeller.

Corn Chowder

Chop a small piece of salt pork and in it fry one sliced onion for five minutes. Strain the browned butter into a saucepan. Parboil four cups of potatoes cut in cubes in boiling water. Drain and put them in the saucepan. Cover with one pint of boiling water, cook till the potatoes are softened, then add one can of chopped corn, one quart of scalded milk, heat to the boiling point. Season with pepper and salt, add three tablespoons of butter and eight crackers which have been soaked in cold milk. A cream corn soup made from chopped corn may be cooked after the directions given for celery soup.

Oyster Soup

Pour a quart of cold water over a pint of oysters. Drain through a colander. Put the water drained from the oysters into a saucepan. Simmer gently three minutes. Remove the scum. Add to the broth in the saucepan one tablespoon each of butter and flour stirred to a paste. Cook three minutes or until smooth, stirring meanwhile. Then add half a cup of unsweetened condensed milk, or common

cream, and season to taste with salt and pepper. When the soup boils, add the drained oysters, and as soon as it again boils and the edges of the oysters curl and separate, remove from the fire and serve.

Cream of Cheese Soup

Heat, but not boil, in a double boiler, one full quart of milk, one blade of mace, one teaspoon of minced onion, one tablespoon of carrot. Blend together one-fourth cup of butter and two level tablespoons of flour. To this add the hot milk, half a cup at a time, stirring constantly and cooking between each addition. Strain back into the double boiler, add three-fourths cup of grated cheese and stir till melted. Season with salt and white pepper and pour over the beaten yolks of two eggs. Cook a moment, remove from the bath and beat with an egg beater till covered with a fine froth. Serve at once in hot cups.—Anne Warner.

Cauliflower Cream Soup

Cook one pint of finely chopped cauliflower in a double boiler with one quart of milk until perfectly tender. Then press through a coarse sieve and return to the fire, season to taste, add one tablespoon of butter and one dessertspoon of cornstarch stirred smoothly in a little cold milk. Cook and stir until perfectly smooth and serve at once with small squares of buttered brown bread.—Mary F. Snider.

Soup as Our Mothers Made It

The day before you want a soup buy a shank of beef. Wash clean and put to cook in two or three gallons of cold water. Bring slowly to a boil. Skim carefully as fast as the scum rises, so that none boils in; cook until the meat slips from the bone. Let the bone remain in the liquor all night and set away in a jar or other earthen vessel to cool; in the morning take off the fat

from the top of the liquor and set it on the stove in your soup kettle. Have ready a large half teacup of whole rice and put it in when you set it to boil, which you must do in season to have three hours before the dinner hour. Wash and scrape two good sized carrots cut in inch pieces, teacup of chopped cabbage, three potatoes and two onions cut small. Boil slowly but constantly on the back of the stove to prevent burning. The rice should dissolve so as to thicken the soup. Just before you dish up add salt, pepper and other seasoning to taste. Keep hot water in the teakettle to add to the soup if needed.—Mrs Sears, Omaha.

Soup Balls

Chop the white meat of a chicken very fine and season highly with salt, pepper, onion juice and a little thyme or curry; add enough yolk of egg to bind together. Roll into very small balls, shake in a plate of flour till covered and poach in boiling water.

Tomato Soup

Into four cups of brown stock put three cups of cold stewed tomato, one stalk of celery, one carrot and one onion chopped, four cloves, four peppercorns and one teaspoon of salt. Allow it to simmer slowly till the tomato is reduced to a pulp. It will take about one hour to cook. Put it in a puree sieve and press all the pulp possible through it. Melt one tablespoon of butter with two tablespoons of flour, add it to the puree and stir, cooking it till smooth. If you dislike the bitter flavor of the tomatoes add half a teaspoon of soda and two teaspoons of sugar before pouring the soup in the tureen. Serve with croutons.

Asparagus Soup

One bundle of asparagus, one pint water, one pint milk or thin cream, one-half an onion, one tablespoon each of butter and flour, salt and pepper to taste. Cut

the heads from the asparagus and cook for twenty minutes in boiling salted water. Cook the stalks and onion in one pint of water for twenty minutes. Rub this through a sieve. Blend butter and flour, add one pint of boiling milk, pepper and salt to taste. Mix with the cooked asparagus and boil for five minutes. Strain again, add the asparagus heads and serve very hot.

Red Bisque with Snowballs

Chop fine one pint each of oysters and clams, add to these and their liquor enough hot water to make two quarts. Add the mashed coral from one lobster, one teaspoon of salt, one-half teaspoon of paprika, a bit of mace, an onion and one tablespoon of Worcestershire sauce, cook three minutes, pour into a sauce made of two tablespoons of butter, two of flour, one and one-half cups of hot milk, and one cup of tomato pulp. When boiling, strain and serve, putting a snow-ball in each plate on its way to the table.

Snowballs

Beat white of one egg, add one cup of whipped cream, season with salt and a few drops of lemon juice, take up with two dessert spoons, forming a ball. The coral and tomatoes will color the soup, and the remainder of the lobster may be used in the salad course.

Black Bean Soup

Soak one pint of black beans over night, in the morning wash and drain them, put in a kettle with two quarts of cold water. In one and one-half table-spoons of butter fry one small onion delicately brown and add to the beans with two stalks of celery broken in pieces. Simmer gently until the beans are quite soft, adding more water if the liquor cooks away. Rub through a sieve, obtaining all the pulp possible; reheat to the boiling point and season with half a teaspoon of salt, one-eighth teaspoon of pepper, a fourth of a tea-

spoon of mustard and a dash of cayenne.
Make a binding from one and a half
tablespoons each of flour and butter
cooked together, and stir into the soup.
Cut two hard-boiled eggs and one lemon
in thin slices, put them in the tureen,
then strain the soup over it and serve.
—Stella A. Downing.

Pea and Bean Purees

An estimate of the food value of these
purees may be inferred from the use
made of these two dried vegetables in
the rations of soldiers and sailors. Soak
the beans or peas (split or Scotch) over
night, then cook to a mush, rub through
a soup strainer, and thin to the proper
consistency with flavored stock. When
unflavored stock is used, add some thyme
to the vegetable while cooking. Add a
little thickening to hold the vegetable
solids in suspension.

A Heavy Vegetable Soup

Put some lean meat two or three times
through a patent chopper (so that it may
be reduced almost to a paste), add cold
water and chopped vegetables, cook
long and slowly, and serve without
straining.

A Nutritious Barley Soup

Prepare lean mutton as in the last
recipe, or leave it on the bone (removing
all fat), add pearl barley, and cook to a
thick puree, in which there should still
be grains that have not lost shape.
Remove bones and large pieces of meat,
and serve without straining.

Velvet Soups

To a quart of strong, well flavored
consomme (beef, chicken, mutton, game,
or "combination") add a large cup of
rich cream which has been poured boiling hot on the beaten yolks of four eggs
mixed with four tablespoons of cold
cream. As a last touch of seasoning,
in reheating, add a little powdered mace.

Boiled chestnuts or blanched almonds,
pounded to a paste, may be added, if
desired.

Vegetable Purees

Cook the vegetable to a mush, rub
through a soup strainer and add the
stock, as in dry bean and pea purees.

Cream Purees

Proceed exactly as in the vegetable
puree, using milk or mixed milk and
cream instead of stock. The thickening
(for holding the solids in suspension) in
cream soups should be made of butter
and flour rubbed to a paste.—Ella Morris
Kretschmar.

Consomme Royale

Have four pounds of shin beef cut into
small pieces. Wash it and place it in a
kettle with four quarts of cold water, and
set the kettle over the fire. Cut into fine
pieces one carrot, one turnip, two small
onions, four sprigs of parsley and two
stalks of celery. Fry them brown in
butter. When the juices are drawn from
the meat, add the vegetables, four teaspoons of salt, one saltspoon of white
pepper and four teaspoons of mixed
herbs (sage, summer savory, marjoram,
bay leaves and thyme), tied up in a bit
of muslin with eight cloves and eight
allspices. Let the water boil, then set
the kettle where it will simmer for six
or seven hours. Strain through a cloth
into a stone jar and let it stand for
twenty-four hours. When ready to
serve, remove the cake of fat from the
top, heat two quarts of the consomme,
color with a little caramel and flavor with
lemon juice and sherry.

Beat two eggs with a spoon, add two
tablespoons of milk, one-fourth teaspoon
of salt and a dash of white pepper. Turn
this into a buttered cup and place it in
the oven in a pan of warm water. Let
it bake until firm in the center when
tried with a knife—from five to ten min-

utes. Cool, cut into small fancy shapes, place in the tureen and pour the boiling soup over the pieces. Serve at once with saltine crackers buttered and browned lightly. To save time in preparation, canned consomme or soup made from beef extract may be used, but it will not have the flavor of the homemade soup stock.—Annabel Lee.

Salmon Bisque

Drain the oil from one-third can of salmon, remove the bones and skin and rub through a sieve. Add gradually one quart of scalded milk, one and a half teaspoons of salt, a dust of pepper, four tablespoons of flour and two tablespoons of butter rubbed into a paste to bind the soup. This is a very nice way to utilize the remains of a can of salmon, remains not large enough to re-serve in any other way. Crab meat or lobster can be made into a bisque in the same way.

Du Barry Soup

Boil one cup of rice in two quarts of clear chicken bouillon, rub through and add one cup of cold cauliflower pressed through a potato ricer. Season with white pepper and salt, add a pint of cream and bring again to the boil. Serve in bouillon cups, garnish with small flowerets of cauliflower.

Rhode Island Chowder

Put into a spider one-third of a cup of fine cubes of fat salt pork, one large onion finely sliced and half a cup of water. Cook till reduced to a small quantity of rich liquor. To four cups of potato cubes which have been parboiled, add this liquor, the strained juice from one quart of clams, the hard portions of the clams finely chopped, and one pint of boiling water. Cook till the potatoes are nearly done, then add one cup of stewed, strained tomato, a quarter of a teaspoon of baking soda and the soft part of the clams. Allow this to simmer gently.

Before pouring the chowder into the tureen, add two cups of scalding milk, two tablespoons of butter, one teaspoon of salt, a dash of pepper and cayenne and a dozen small crackers.

Fish Chowder

Cut three pounds of any kind of fresh fish (codfish is especially good), one and one-half pounds of potatoes and one large onion into slices; and half a pound of salt pork into half-inch squares or dice. Put the pork and onions into a saucepan and fry them a light brown; then add a cup of claret, and when it boils take it from the fire. Butter a large stewpan and put in first a layer of potatoes, then a layer of fish, then a sprinkle of onions and pork (strained from the claret), pepper and salt, and continue these alternations until it is all in, having the potatoes on top. Now pour the claret over the top and barely cover the whole with boiling water. Cover closely and let it simmer for fifteen minutes without disturbing it.

Corn Soup

Stew two chickens, or if preferred, a knuckle of veal. Grate twelve ears of uncooked corn. When the meat is tender, lift it out of the broth and to the latter add the grated corn and a teaspoon of tapioca farina. Cook for half an hour, then add pepper, salt, a little chopped parsley and a hard-boiled egg chopped fine. Make a thickening of three tablespoons of flour and add five minutes before serving the soup.

Mock Bisque Soup

One quart of tomatoes cooked tender in one quart of water. Strain this and put the liquor back upon the stove; add one teaspoon of soda, a little butter, salt and pepper to taste, and, just before it is served, one quart of boiling milk. A little thickening and onion improves it for some tastes.—Mrs C. B. Stoddard.

Tapioca Cream Soup

One quart of white stock, one pint of cream or milk, one onion, two stalks of celery, one-third cup of tapioca, two cups of cold water, one tablespoon of butter, small piece of mace, salt, pepper. Wash the tapioca and soak. Cook it and the stock together, very gently, for one hour. Cut the onion and celery into small pieces, and put on to cook for twenty minutes with the milk and mace. Strain on the tapioca and stock. Season, add butter and serve.—B. C. J

Noodles

Noodles are an excellent accompaniment to soup and very easily made. Beat one egg slightly, add half a teaspoon of salt, then work in as much flour as the wetting will take up. Knead it well, toss on a floured board and roll out as thin as a sheet of paper. Cover with a towel and set aside for twenty minutes. Cut into fancy shapes with French vegetable cutters. There may be diamonds, hearts, clover leaves or circles. The sheet may be shredded finely with a sharp vegetable knife or rolled like a jelly roll and cut into the finest shavings. Set aside to dry and use when required, cooking the noodles for twenty minutes before they are needed in boiling salted water. Drain and add to the soup just before sending to the table. Noodles may also be cooked in stock, seasoned and served as a side dish.—See Page XIX.

Vegetables

Potatoes in the Half Shell

Bake six medium-sized potatoes; when they are soft cut a slice from the top of each and scoop out the potato. Mash it, add two tablespoons of butter, salt, pepper, two tablespoons of hot milk and the whites of two eggs beaten stiff. Put this mixture back into the skins, sprinkle with grated cheese and bake for five minutes in a very hot oven.

Baked Stuffed Peppers

Cut green peppers in two lengthwise. Remove the seeds and let the peppers soak in cold water for half an hour. Dry them and fill with a stuffing made of bread crumbs, chopped meat and seasoning—pepper, salt, sage and onion juice to taste. Place them in a pan and bake until brown on top. Add a little soup stock or melted butter and hot water before placing in the oven. Serve hot with fish or meat.

Boiled Onions

Pour boiling water over the onions and remove the skins. Cook them for five minutes in boiling salted water, then change the water and change again in ten minutes, to remove the strong taste. Boil until tender, about one-half hour, then drain off the water, season with salt, butter and pepper and add one cup or more of cream sauce. Cook for ten minutes and serve in a deep covered vegetable dish.—Annabel Lee.

Scalloped Potatoes

Slice, after paring, raw potatoes enough to fill a deep baking dish full, shaking them down well. Put the potatoes in the dish in layers, with bits of

butter, salt and pepper until full. Pour
over a cup of milk and put in the oven
to bake. It will take at least an hour to
bake. If the oven is quick, cover at first.
If milk dries away, add more. The more
butter and baking, the better the dish.
A few slices of salt pork may be laid
over the top with less butter; if pork is
not liked, remove just before potatoes
are done. A little onion juice is liked
by some.

Baked Cabbage and Bacon

Shred or chop coarse three pounds of
cabbage. Stir into it a tablespoon of
flour, a teaspoon of salt, the same of
sifted dry mustard, a little paprika and
half a cup of water. Put into a granite
baking dish, lay over the top six thin
slices of lean bacon, and cover tight.
Bake in a hot oven an hour in summer
time, longer in winter. If it does not
brown with the cover on, remove for a
few minutes. The bacon is nice, how-
ever, if a thin tin is used for cover and
not removed.

Baked Brown Potatoes

Boil, peel and mash a dozen potatoes.
Beat into them, while hot, salt and pepper to taste, a spoonful of onion juice,
half a cup of milk and a tablespoon of
butter. Have them perfectly smooth
and creamy. Butter a long, shallow
cake tin, and fill evenly with the potato,
bake brown in a hot oven, cut out like a
johnnycake and serve with luncheon or
supper.

Frijoles (Spanish Beans) with Cheese

Boil one pint of pink beans in plenty
of cold water. As water boils away, add
more (hot) water until beans are very
tender. Season to taste with salt and
red pepper. Put in frying pan a heaping
tablespoon of lard and butter (half of
each). When the beans are very hot in
the pot, put in one small onion and mash

them a little with a spoon, then put them into the boiling grease. Stir well, and allow to brown slightly. Ten minutes before taking from the frying pan, add seven tablespoons of grated American cheese. Serve with slices of hot buttered toast (thin) and sliced cucumbers with French dressing.—Margaret Greenleaf, Pasadena.

Browned Sweet Potatoes

Boil the potatoes until they can be pierced with a fork, but not until tender. Remove the skins, dust lightly with sugar, roll in melted butter and brown in the oven.

Buttered Cauliflower

Break a firm head of cauliflower into sprigs and cook in boiling water until about half done. Take up, drain, and put into a saucepan with two tablespoons of melted butter, the juice of one lemon, two tablespoons of white sauce or of cream, a pinch of cayenne, a little salt, and a small cup of hot water. Cook until tender, take up, strain the gravy, add to it one cup of cream or white sauce, pour over the cauliflower, and serve at once.—Mary Foster Snider.

Southern Sweet Potatoes

Boil six medium-sized sweet potatoes until nearly done. Peel and slice the long way into pieces about half an inch thick. Fill a baking dish with layers of the slices thickly covered with dark brown sugar and bits of butter. Pour over a half cup of boiling water. Cook in a hot oven for twenty or thirty minutes. This will fill a quart and a half baking dish.—Mrs Henry S. Judson.

Sweet Potato Croquettes

To two cups of hot riced sweet potatoes add three tablespoons of butter, one-half teaspoon of salt, few grains of pepper and one beaten egg. Shape, roll in flour, egg and crumbs, fry in deep fat and drain.

If the potatoes are very dry it will be necessary to add a small amount of milk to moisten.

Corn Oysters

Scrape sweet corn from the cob, or grate it. Take one coffeecup of corn and two eggs. Make a batter of a little milk and flour, seasoning with salt. Make the batter sufficiently thick to take out with a spoon, and fry in butter. This recipe is enough for five persons.—Mrs William Edwards.

Mashed Turnips

Select the large yellow turnips, as they are sweetest. The Cape Cod turnip is a good kind. Wash, pare and cut them into pieces. Boil them in salted boiling water until tender. Drain, mash, season with butter, pepper and salt, and heap lightly in a vegetable dish.—A. Lee.

Boiled Cauliflower

Remove the outer leaves and cut off the stem close to the flowers. Wash thoroughly in cold water and soak in cold salted water (top downward) for one hour, allowing one tablespoon of salt to one gallon of water. Then tie it in a piece of muslin or cheesecloth to keep it whole and cook it in slightly salted boiling water until tender, keeping it closely covered. When done, lift it from the water, remove the cloth, stand it in a round dish with the flowers up, pour cream sauce over it and serve at once.—M. F. S.

Scalloped Cauliflower

Break the cauliflower into small sprigs and cook in boiling salted water until tender. Place the pieces in a buttered pudding dish and pour over them a sauce made as follows: Mix well together one-half pint of bread crumbs, one pint of sweet milk, one beaten egg, two teaspoons of salt and a little pepper. Bake until

slightly browned. One cup of diced chicken or veal added to the sauce makes a great improvement. When this is used allow an extra cup of milk and a little more seasoning.—M. F. S.

Savory Cauliflower

Cook the cauliflower as in above recipes and set aside to cool. Prepare a pint of egg batter and add to it a teaspoon of minced parsley and a tablespoon of grated mild cheese. Dip each sprig of cauliflower in this batter and fry in butter. When done place on a hot dish and serve at once.

Fricassee of Parsnips

Scrape the parsnips and boil them in milk until tender. Take out and cut them in four pieces if they are large; add a piece of butter the size of a walnut, also salt and pepper to the milk they were boiled in, thicken with a very little cornstarch or flour; put the parsnips back in the dressing and let them simmer about forty minutes.—Mrs Sada Ballard.

Asparagus Tips in Croustades

These are nice served with broiled chicken or chops, or as a separate course following the meat. The croustades can be prepared in advance and heated in a quick oven when wanted. Trim slices of bread two inches thick free from crusts. Cut into squares three or four inches in size. With a pointed knife take from the center as much crumb as possible, leaving a small square box. Fry a golden brown in a kettle of hot fat; drain. Fill the centers with asparagus tips in any good sauce, or a well made cream sauce.

Asparagus Cream Omelet

Stir one heaping tablespoon of butter and same amount of flour together. Set the saucepan over the fire, and when well blended, add one cup of milk; stir until smooth, add a teaspoon of chopped pars-

ley, remove from the fire and cool. Beat three eggs separately, the whites to a stiff froth; add the yolks to the cold sauce with a teaspoon of salt and a dash of cayenne; add also one cup of cooked asparagus tips and the stiffly beaten whites. Put a tablespoon of butter in a hot frying pan. When it is brown, pour in the mixture, break it in places with a fork to allow the uncooked portion to run down. When it is set, place in a hot oven for five minutes, double over and serve.

Asparagus Loaf with Yellow Bechamel Sauce

Butter thoroughly a charlotte mold, quart size, and line it with cooked tips of asparagus well drained. Cook two tablespoons of flour and two tablespoons of butter together, add a teaspoon of salt, a dash of cayenne and one cup of cream gradually. Allow it to boil five minutes, remove from the fire, add one cup of cooked asparagus tips and four eggs thoroughly beaten. Turn the mixture carefully into the decorated mold, set the mold into a pan of hot water and cook in a moderate oven about thirty minutes, or until the center is firm. Turn the loaf onto a dish, arrange about it little triangular pieces of bread that have been dipped in beaten egg and milk and browned in hot butter. Pour around the sauce and serve at once.

Yellow Bechamel Sauce

Mix two tablespoons of flour and two of butter, cook until it begins to bubble, add gradually half a cup of hot stock and half a cup of milk. When the sauce boils, set into a dish of hot water and stir in the beaten yolks of two eggs, half a cup of cooked asparagus tips, a teaspoon of salt, a dash of cayenne and a tablespoon of lemon juice. In place of stock the water in which the asparagus was cooked may be used. This sauce is excellent

served with broiled cutlets or with
warmed-over meats. In this case add an
extra half cup of asparagus tips.—E. M.
Lucas.

Peeled and Curried Tomatoes

Cut four large tomatoes into rather
thick slices. Saute them in one and one-
half tablespoons of butter. When nearly
cooked sprinkle with one teaspoon of
curry powder, one tablespoon of flour,
one teaspoon of finely chopped onion, a
dash of salt and pepper. At the last minute add one cup of cream, let it boil up
and then strain over the tomatoes served
on buttered rounds of toast.

Tomatoes with Spaghetti Stuffing

Scoop the inside from eight tomatoes.
To one and a half cups of cooked
spaghetti add the tomato pulp, one
tablespoon of butter, pepper, salt and a
few drops of onion juice. Fill each
tomato cover with buttered crumbs and
bake till brown. Instead of preparing
the spaghetti, a left-over of spaghetti or
macaroni slightly chopped may be very
savorily utilized for this dish.

Cauliflower au Gratin

Boil the cauliflower. Melt a tablespoon of butter in a saucepan and stir
smoothly in one tablespoon of flour, thin
with half a pint of milk, stir until boiling, add four tablespoons of grated
cheese, a dash of cayenne and salt to
taste. Pour this over the cauliflower
and serve hot.—M. F. S.

Baked Tomatoes, Creole Style

Cut into two halves crosswise, six fine
large tomatoes, place them in a buttered
baking pan and sprinkle over them two
green peppers finely chopped, one teaspoon of chopped onion, two tablespoons of butter in small morsels and a
liberal seasoning of salt and paprika.
Lift the tomato slices carefully onto

rounds of buttered toast, then add to the
liquor left in the baking pan two tablespoons of butter and two tablespoons of
flour melted and browned, stir well with
a wire whisk, add one cup of cream, let
it boil up, then strain over the tomatoes
and toast.—M. F. S.

Scalloped Tomatoes

Scald and peel half a dozen tomatoes,
set them in a buttered baking dish, sprinkle with pepper, salt and a dust of powdered sugar. Cover with buttered dry
crumbs and bake till brown.

Tomatoes Stuffed

Cut a thin slice off the tops of eight
large, firm tomatoes and with a spoon
carefully lift out the pulp. Rub it
through a sieve, discarding the seeds.
To the juice add half a cup of stale bread
crumbs, two tablespoons of melted butter, a dust of salt, pepper and paprika
and half a teaspoon of minced parsley.
Stuff the tomato shells with this, put a
bit of butter on top of each and set in a
hot oven for ten minutes.

Stuffed Spanish Onions

Peel the onions under water and
scoop out from the top a portion of the
center. Parboil five minutes and turn
upside down to drain. Make a stuffing
of the chopped onion taken from the
centers, softened bread crumbs, salt, pepper and a generous amount of butter.
Fill the onions heaping full and sprinkle
the top with buttered crumbs. Cover
and cook till tender (about an hour) in
a pan containing a small quantity of
water. Let them brown a very little
before taking from the oven.

Cold Slaw

Chop with one small head of cabbage
two hard-boiled eggs. Take one-half
cup of sour cream, one tablespoon of
sugar, a little salt and pepper, and a tea-

spoon of celery seed; beat all together, then add one teacup of vinegar, and pour over the cabbage. If this is put in a tight vessel, it will keep several days.—Mrs Creigh, Omaha.

Potato Puff

Soak old potatoes for several hours and boil in salted water. To two cups of potato mashed or put through a ricer add two tablespoons of butter, one teaspoon of salt and a little white pepper; fold in the whites of two eggs whipped stiff. Bake in a buttered dish.—Anne Warner.

Savory Carrots

Scrape, then cut new carrots into straws. Cook tender in salted water and drain dry. Season with salt, pepper and a little onion juice and return to the kettle with a generous piece of butter and shake till hot and glazed. Pile on a dish in pyramid form, add a cup of fresh green peas well seasoned and a sprinkling of chopped parsley.—Anne Warner.

Maitre d'Hotel Potatoes

Wash, pare and cut potatoes into balls, using a French vegetable cutter, making two cups. Soak fifteen minutes in cold water and cook in boiling salted water until soft. Drain and add the sauce. For this, cream three tablespoons of butter, add one teaspoon of lemon juice, one-half teaspoon of salt, one-eighth teaspoon of pepper and one-half tablespoon of finely chopped parsley.—Stella A. Downing.

Spinach Croquettes

Take one pint of spinach (cooked), chop very fine. Put over the fire one large tablespoon of butter and one-half of a small onion cut in quarters. When the onion colors, remove the pieces and put the spinach in, stirring constantly, and adding gradually one scant table-

spoon of flour, same of bread crumbs, one-half cup of grated cheese, yolks of two eggs beaten and stirred in quickly, one-fourth cup of milk (more, if too stiff), salt and nutmeg to taste. It must only be stiff enough to mold while warm. Turn out on a floured board; flour the hands and form into small croquettes. Then cook them in boiling lard from five to seven minutes. Shake or drain in a sieve. Arrange them in the dish in which they are to be served, sprinkle with grated cheese, moisten with melted butter, and place in oven a minute or two to heat through.—Mrs Peter C. Corwell.

Creamed Carrots

Scrape the carrots and cut in slices one-fourth of an inch thick. Let them lie in cold water an hour before cooking. Boil till tender in salted water, drain and pour over them a well seasoned white sauce.

Turnip Ragout

Melt three tablespoons of butter, when hot add one quart of finely sliced raw turnip with one tablespoon of finely chopped onion. Cook slowly on the back of the stove till tender. Add one teaspoon of sugar, one teaspoon of salt and two tablespoons of flour. Cook two minutes, then add one cup of milk.

Deviled Tomatoes

For this dish **use** six large, solid tomatoes. Wipe, peel and cut in slices half an inch thick. Dust with pepper, salt and flour and saute in brown butter. Lift each slice carefully with a skimmer when cooked and lay on a hot platter. Pour over them a sauce made as follows: Cream half a cup of butter, add four teaspoons of powdered sugar, two teaspoons of mustard, half a teaspoon of salt, a dust of cayenne, the yolks of two hard-boiled eggs rubbed to a paste, two eggs beaten slightly and a quarter of a

cup of vinegar. While the tomatoes
saute put the sauce to cook in a bowl set
in a teakettle—the double boiler is too
hot for it—and pour when thickened over
the sauted tomatoes.

Broiled Tomatoes

For this dish choose tomatoes which
are not dead ripe. Cut them unpeeled in
rather thick slices. Dust with pepper,
salt and powdered sugar, roll in hot
melted butter, then in finely sifted bread
crumbs and brown in a wire broiler over
a clear fire. This dish has a delicious
flavor if instead of rolling in butter the
slices of tomato are dipped in rich oil
mayonnaise.

Tomato Farcies

Scoop out the tomato pulp, leaving the
shells, and fill with a stuffing made from
half a cup of sausage meat, four tablespoons of stale bread crumbs, one teaspoon of minced parsley, a shred of garlic,
one teaspoon of tarragon vinegar and one
teaspoon of finely minced onion. Set the
tomatoes in a baking dish, cover with buttered bread crumbs and bake till chest-
nut brown. Just before sending to the
table squeeze over them the juice of one
lemon.

Peas in Turnip Cups

Steam small white turnips, hollow out
the centers, cut the edges in points.
Fill with peas which have been heated
in a sauce made of two tablespoons of
butter cooked with two tablespoons of
flour, one cup of milk and one-fourth teaspoon of salt. Serve hot.—See Page
XVII.

Corn Timbales

Score six ears of sweet corn and press
out the pulp. To one cup add one tablespoon of butter melted, half teaspoon of
salt, one-fourth teaspoon of Hungarian
paprika, the beaten yolks of three eggs,

then the stiffly-beaten whites and one tablespoon of flour; butter corn timbale molds, then fill with the mixture two-thirds full; set in a pan of water and place in hot oven; bake until firm; un-mold onto a hot plate.—See Page XX.

Index